I0879878

THE UNIVERSITY OF MICHIGAN
CENTER FOR JAPANESE STUDIES

MICHIGAN PAPERS IN JAPANESE STUDIES
NO. 5

# CULTURE AND RELIGION IN JAPANESE-AMERICAN RELATIONS: ESSAYS ON UCHIMURA KANZŌ, 1861-1930

Edited by

Ray A. Moore

Ann Arbor

Center for Japanese Studies
The University of Michigan

1981

Library of Congress Cataloging in Publication Data

Main entry under title:

Culture and religion in Japanese-American relations.

(Michigan Papers in Japanese studies; no. 5)
Bibliography: pp. 137-142
1. Uchimura, Kanzō, 1861-1930--Addresses, essays, lectures. I. Moore, Ray A., 1933- . II. Series.
BV4935.U25C84 280'.4'0924 81-21966
ISBN 0-939512-10-6

Printed in the United States of America

## TABLE OF CONTENTS

To all the Uchimura Fellows
of Amherst College

## Preface

The inspiration for this collection of essays on Uchimura Kanzō was Ōyama Tsunao, a young professor of Hokusei Gakuen College in Sapporo, who came to Amherst College on a Fulbright grant in 1976-77. Professor Ishida Takeshi, Tokyo University, who was also visiting the U.S. at that time, had agreed to give a lecture on Uchimura in the spring of 1977. Professor Ōyama suggested a seminar instead of the usual public lecture. I agreed to organize the meeting and to seek support from Amherst College, and invited as a third participant Professor Ohara Shin who was at Harvard that year and whose book, Hyōden Uchimura Kanzō, had just appeared. When the quality of the three papers became apparent, I proposed publication and sought out other scholars who were conducting research on Uchimura--Professors Robert Lee, Hirakawa Sukehiro, Ōta Yūzō and Carlo Caldarola--to contribute to the project. Most of the editing was completed during the summer of 1978 after Professor Richard K. Beardsley, Director of the Center for the Japanese Studies at the Univesity of Michigan, encouraged me to submit the essays for publication in the Center's Occasional Papers. However, the Center's decision to reevaluate its Occasional Papers and Professor Beardsley's untimely death some months later combined to delay the project until the summer of 1980.

I wish to thank the contributors to this collection for their patience and understanding while the project languished for nearly two years. The original seminar would not have been possible without the customary sympathetic support of Amherst College and the then Dean of the Faculty, Prosser Gifford, now Associate Director of the Wilson Center in Washington, D.C. I would like to take this opportunity to express my gratitude for his support for this and other projects over the years. Professor John Howes of British Columbia University, the foremost American authority on Uchimura, kindly suggested the names of several contributors even though his own tight schedule would not allow him to prepare an essay for the collection. In Japan I must acknowledge a special debt of gratitude to my senior colleague Otis Cary, professor of history and Amherst's representative at Dōshisha University, for much wise advice over the years and, especially, for sending me in the summer of 1978 to a bookstore in the Hongō section of Tokyo. The owner, Mr. Shinagawa Tsutome, not only had recently revised his exhaustive bibliography on Uchimura, but was willing to share with me his rich knowledge of Uchimura and his followers, and to ride his bicycle across the city to the International House in Roppongi to deliver several books on Uchimura before I returned to the United States. To Frost Library at Amherst College goes my thanks for permission to use the Uchimura Kanzō, Niishima Jō, and Julius H. Seelye papers.

I am pleased to acknowledge the assistance of Jean Dunbar who kept her sense of humor while typing and retyping the manuscript; my two sons, Mark and Kenneth, for compiling the bibliography and helping with the proofreading; and especially, my wife, Ilga, who is equal to any task anytime.

Macrons have been used where appropriate to indicate long vowels in Japanese words save the most familiar proper nouns. Japanese names are given in the customary Japanese manner, with the family name preceding the personal one, except for some publications in Western languages where, for example, Uchimura Kanzō is called Kanzō Uchimura. Variant readings of Niishima Jō (e.g., Niijima Jō, Joseph Hardy Neesima, Neesima Shimeta) have been corrected, except in Western language publications in the bibliography.

Readers unfamiliar with the major events of Japanese history during the late nineteenth and early twentieth centuries may wish to begin with Robert Lee's essay, which provides more historical background on the events of Uchimura's life than the other essays do.

Ray A. Moore<br>July 1980<br>Amherst College

# INTRODUCTION

Ray A. Moore

The seven essays in this volume offer an evaluation of Uchimura Kanzō (1861-1930), one of modern Japan's most enigmatic intellectuals, who has enjoyed something of a renaissance in postwar Japan. Together they provide new insights into Uchimura's development and his influence on his countrymen and on Japanese-American relations. There are two reasons for undertaking to publish a collection of essays of this kind. First, there is a paucity of studies in English on a man who, it is generally agreed, was a significant figure in modern Japan's intellectual history. Despite the pioneering work of John Howes, whose many articles are included in the attached bibliography, not a single published volume is presently available in English on Uchimura Kanzō. The second reason is more personal. Uchimura was one of the early Japanese graduates of Amherst College (class of 1887) to achieve national and international prominence. Having taught East Asian history at Amherst since 1965, I am keenly aware of the strong ties which Uchimura, Niishima Jō and other young Japanese of the late nineteenth century forged not only between Amherst and Japan but between the United States and Japan.

I propose in this brief introduction (1) to call attention to one significant theme in several of the essays, and (2) to identify the major contribution of each essay to an exploration of that theme. Because of my own current research on postwar Japan, I am drawn to the notion of Uchimura as a model—an indigenous model—of individualism in postwar Japan. Under the pressure of the American Occupation, many Japanese searched their own modern history for an exemplar of the personal qualities which they considered essential to the development of a "spirit of democracy" in Japanese society. Such Uchimura followers as Takagi Yasaka, for instance, called attention in the 1940's and 1950's to the fierce independence and individualism that had characterized his whole life. He was a Christian, a pacifist, a powerful advocate of democracy; but he was also a patriot, and often a vociferous critic of the United States and other western nations. What Japan needed in the postwar period, Takagi suggested, was Uchimura's independence of spirit, which was ultimately derived from his religion, Protestant Christianity.

In a moment of national humiliation after defeat in the war, Japan's leaders did express an interest in the victor's religion. In September 1945 Prime Minister Higashikuni said that Japan needed Christianity and the inspiration of Jesus Christ. General MacArthur and his staff obliged by encouraging foreign missionaries to return to Japan and spread the Christian gospel. Prominent Christians served in early postwar cabinets and held other high positions in government. Members of the Imperial family took Bible lessons and learned to sing Christian hymns; Imperial princes attended Christian churches openly; and rumor had it that even the Emperor was contemplating a conversion to Christianity. The perception soon spread among Americans that Christianity was taking hold in "heathen" Japan. The skeptic might argue that the interest was more apparent than real, that it was artificially stimulated by conditions of defeat and foreign military occupation. The skeptic would be right. Few Japanese sincerely believed, as MacArthur did, that democracy could only flourish where Christian principles prevailed. Yet many of them did suspect that individualism was an essential ingredient of democracy, and that Christianity might be important in developing a stronger sense of individuality in Japanese society. As both Robert Lee and Ōta Yūzō point out in their essays, many Japanese shared a vague belief that Uchimura could serve as a model of individualism that was generally lacking among the Japanese.

The appearance in the 1950s of Uchimura's collected works and studies by Masaike Jin and Suzuki Toshirō aroused considerable interest in a Christian who exemplified loyalty to both "Christ and country." Here was a Japanese who could advocate democracy, pacifism, and personal independence without appearing to denigrate his own past or to embrace the complete westernization of Japan or show personal subservience to Americans. The defeat and foreign occupation had posed again the painful dilemma: how to be both Japanese and modern, or in postwar terms, how to recover a healthy pride in one's national and cultural heritage while living with the radical changes imposed by American military fiat. I would argue that this dilemma goes far in explaining the interest in Uchimura during the 1950s and 1960s, an interest which continues today. To many, Uchimura had shown how one could be a patriot and a very "Japanese" person who maintained pride in his own cultural tradition while being loyal to a set of values derived from Christianity. This appealed emotionally to Japanese who had been force-fed through education and the mass media a massive dose of Americanism. Perhaps through Uchimura's experience they too could learn how to live with pride and confidence in a Japan being transformed by outside forces.

The authors of the following essays are representative of the current scholarship on Uchimura and his Japanese Christianity known as Mukyōkai. As their footnotes indicate, several of them have recently completed substantial studies dealing with Uchimura--Ōta, Ohara, Hirakawa, and Lee critical biographies, and Caldarola a sociological analysis of Mukyōkai. The essays presented here give a good sense of the richness and variety of the studies and interpretations that have become available in recent years. Several of the essays raise questions about Uchimura's view of his society and his strongly ambivalent feelings about the west. While confirming his stubborn independence, they suggest that his actions were often those of one deeply alienated from both the cultures of which he was part.

In the first essay, Ishida Takeshi, writing on the concept of independence in Uchimura's thought, cautions against judging him for what he did not pretend to be. "We should be careful," he writes, "not to expect what we cannot and should not expect of him." His mission was to dissent, not to be a model of anything. He chose to be in the minority. His rejection of both Japan's imperial orthodoxy and the established Christian church made him an heretic. Ishida traces the evolution of his heretical thought by focusing on the key concept of independence as he recounts several major incidents in Uchimura's life. His radical understanding of independence ("Standing directly with God and truth") meant freedom from man, government, and temple or church. His strict application of this concept in his own life led him to reject all institutions, including even attempts to perpetuate the meetings of his Bible classes in Mukyōkai groups. His analysis led in the end to a sense of hopelessness and despair over politics and international affairs. Uchimura emerges from Ishida's essay not as hero or villain but as a tragic figure whose deep sense of despair and militant religious belief would allow no compromise and no tranquility even in the waning years of his life. Ishida concludes, however, that this prophet of national doom and his Mukyōkai followers have played "an important role as political dissenters" in modern Japanese history.

Doi Takeo has pointed out in a recent study of Uchimura the influence which several strong personalities exercised on him in his early years. At home his mother rather than his father was the dominant force. During his years of education several of the strongest figures in his life were foreigners--William S. Clark (though he had no direct personal contact with Clark), Julius H. Seelye, David Bell, and Thomas Carlyle. The next three essays illustrate just how deeply such men influenced his life. Educated almost entirely in English, Uchimura carried on extensive correspondence in this foreign language with Seelye and Bell and even with his Japanese friends from Sapporo days. Ōyama and Moore show in their brief essay on Uchimura at Amherst in 1885-87 the powerful influence which Julius Seelye exercised on him. His own background, his age, and his brooding temperament effectively isolated him from the other students at Amherst. They were the younger generation of Americans who did not fully share the puritanical fervor of clergyman and college president Seelye. Consequently, Uchimura never fully comprehended either the strong secular trends among the younger generation of Americans or the changes going on in American education during his years at Amherst. Therefore, the effect of his Amherst education was, on the one hand, a deepening religious commitment under Seelye's tutelage and, on the other, a growing suspicion of American society and churches. One reinforced the other as Uchimura internalized Seelye's doubts about modern American society along with his own.

One result of his nearly four years in the United States was a growing bitterness about American society which he expressed in his first book, How I Became a Christian. Hirakawa Sukehiro's essay provides an extended analysis of Uchimura's "ambivalent and seemingly contradictory feelings about the United States." He points to the racism which the young Japanese encountered and to his defense of poor Chinese immigrants, while showing irritation at being identified as a "Chinaman." Likewise, while denouncing the ills of American industrial society, he expressed pride in Japan's own rapid industrialization. Hirakawa sees Uchimura's anti-American rhetoric as a product, ironically, of his Christian background which, as Ōyama and Moore also hint, provided an idealistic, ethical standard to which the real America did not measure up. Despite his strong anti-American feelings, Uchimura maintained close ties with some Americans through much of his life, and his later symbolic "return to Japan" was never complete, for, as Hirakawa says, his "Christian faith had penetrated . . . too deeply for that."

The third major foreign influence on Uchimura came from the writings of Thomas Carlyle (1795-1881). Uchimura found a special resonance in this irascible Scotsman. He cheered as he read Carlyle's denunciation of society and the world; and he drew strength from Carlyle's writings as he himself struggled to become a writer in Kyoto in 1893. As Ōta Yūzō explains in his study, Carlyle's writings gave Uchimura the confidence to believe in the value of what he himself wrote. Ōta shows through a close examination of Uchimura's early writings that Carlyle left a deep impression on his style as well as his thought. One of Uchimura's first successful essays, "Jisei no kansatsu" (The Signs of the Times), published in Kokumin no tomo in 1896, was inspired by his reading of Carlyle's essay of the same title. Uchimura saw in

Carlyle a mirror image of himself—a strong individual struggling "in a corrupt and hostile world." Ōta argues that indeed the influence may have been too great. Under his spell, Uchimura's discontent grew; and he alienated friends by trying to make "his mistaken ideas pass for truth," as Arishima Takeo put it. Carlyle's example encouraged him to be quarrelsome, egotistical, and arrogant. The result was not altogether pleasant as the man exalted "his own narrowness." Ōta thus expresses strong disagreement with those who would see Uchimura as a healthy example of individualism in postwar Japan.

In his essay Robert Lee explores the tension between Uchimura's strong sense of service to Christ and country. Throughout his life, Lee argues, this struggle went on. Lee applies Kenneth Pyle's concept of the "new generation" of Meiji Japan to Uchimura. His "search for meaning" in his life involved, as it did for Shiga Shigetake and other members of the new generation, a definition of Japan as a nation and culture and its place in a world shaped largely by the western powers. But unlike Shiga, Miyake Setsurei and even Tokutomi Sohō, Uchimura found no solace, no release from doubt, and no resolution of the uncertainty about his own cultural and personal identity in Japan's victories over China and Russia. On the contrary, both events plunged him more deeply into doubt about the future of his country. In Lee's analysis Uchimura's growing disillusionment, which was brought on as much by personal relations as by his Christian standards or the failure of his country to live up to those standards, was a powerful force in his search for purpose and meaning in life.

The last two essays by Carlo Caldarola and Ohara Shin explore the influence of Uchimura's thought through the non-church Christian movement which he inspired. Both essays raise stimulating questions about the relationship between culture and religion as seen in the Mukyōkai movement. Caldarola sees Mukyōkai as a case of "selective indigenization of Christianity in Japan" in which the "essential aspects of both cultures" (Japan and the west) are combined "to produce a new culture." While such a statement does not address directly the issue raised by Ōta, it does imply that Uchimura was successful in blending the two cultures into a form acceptable to many Japanese rather than being alienated from both. Caldarola's analysis of Mukyōkai suggests that its protestant and puritanical spirit, which appeals to Japanese intellectuals, has radical implications for society since it inspires them to engage in political and social dissent against the corrupting influences of the church and other institutions. He points to a source of pride for many Japanese in Mukyōkai's assumption that Asians are better prepared to bring about a second reformation to achieve the ultimate Protestant goal of a communion of free souls. He argues that basic cultural differences between

Japan and the west account for the growth of Mukyōkai which is "truly congenial" with the Japanese concept of religion as an "intensive spontaneous experience of the individual soul" and with the traditional particularistic pattern of Japanese social relations.

Ohara's analysis is essentially in agreement with Caldarola's, i.e., that Mukyōkai's emphasis on loose group formations is consistent with Japanese cultural principles that stress the personal and informal relationship. Ohara's major contribution, however, is his stimulating speculation on the possibility of cross cultural experience for "churchless Americans" in the Mukyōkai Christianity which Uchimura inspired. Reviewing the principal events of Uchimura's life, Ohara notes the special meaning which Uchimura attached to Mukyōkai and his consistent resistance to church organization, clergy and missionaries. The Bible is the sole authority for Mukyōkai Christians; no one is ordained, and anybody is free to form his own Bible study meetings. He points out interesting parallels between Mukyōkai and the existential Christian movement in contemporary American society. The many Americans who now find themselves in a "church-less situation", or alienated from their church and engaged in a spiritual quest, might find in Mukyōkai, Ohara suggests, a way of maintaining their faith without a church affiliation, for despite its Japanese origins Mukyōkai is "universally applicable."

No set of relatively brief papers can hope to capture the full complexity of Uchimura and his thought. The purpose of these essays is not to offer a general interpretation but simply to suggest the rich variety that is possible. If they succeed in that modest aim, they will nonetheless have made a contribution to a better understanding of Uchimura and his role in the history of Japanese-American cultural relations.

# THE MEANING OF "INDEPENDENCE" IN THE THOUGHT OF UCHIMURA KANZŌ

Ishida Takeshi

Uchimura Kanzō, who was born in 1861, seven years before the Meiji Restoration, and who died some seventy years later, in 1930, on the eve of the militarist era in Japan, has often been depicted as a steadfast opponent of Japanese nationalist ideology. Disciples and admirers, pointing to his stand against imperial ideology in the famous lese majesty incident in 1891, and recalling his pacifist attitude toward the Russo-Japanese War, assume that from the beginning of his adult life, Uchimura rebelled against the emperor system. This view of Uchimura's life neglects the historical development of his thought as a heretic.[1]

Those who have a historical perspective on Uchimura's life and thought fall into other errors of distortion. One writer holds Uchimura partly responsible for the "failure of freedom" in Japan, because Uchimura assumed an apolitical stance in the latter half of his life, instead of actively attempting to implement democratic reforms.[2] Some historians, separating this apolitical stance of Uchimura's later years from the radical socio-political criticism that characterizd his thought around the turn of the century, indicate simply that Uchimura's interest in social problems faded.[3]

1. One such example is: Suzuki Toshirō (ed.), Uchimura Kanzō to gendai (Uchimura Kanzō and the present), Iwanami Shoten, 1961.
2. See, for example, Tatsuo Arima, The Failure of Freedom: A portrait of Modern Japanese Intellectuals (Harvard University Press, 1969), Chap. 2.
3. See, for example, Ienaga Saburō, "Nihon shisōshijō no Uchimura Kanzō (Uchimura Kanzō in the History of Japanese Thought)" in Suzuki Toshirō, ed., Kaisō no Uchimura Kanzō (Reminiscences of Uchimura Kanzō), Iwanami Shoten, 1956, pp. 114ff.

Nobody can deny the historical significance of Uchimura Kanzō's critical attitude toward the reality of modernizing Japan. However, this critical posture should be understood in terms of its origins and development. In this paper, I should like to trace the evolution of Uchimura's heretical thought by focusing on one key theme, his concept of independence.

Uchimura Kanzō did not consciously set out to be a rebel; rather, to borrow his own words, he was "impelled" by circumstances or by the "will of God."[4] This does not mean that his own will did not play a siginificant role. Whenever he stood at a crossroads, he always chose the more difficult and less popular way. In his interpretation of samurai ethics, the difficult way was the noble way. Depending upon nothing but God's will, he welcomed challenges that required him to fight alone. As a result, despite his loyalty to Japan, he became a traitor in the eyes of Japanese nationalists, and, despite his strong belief in God, he became Satan in the eyes of Japanese Christians. A heretic to both nationalists and Christians alike, Uchimura was forced to endure isolation and ostracism, and out of this lonely experience, he forged his principle of independence.

The first time he asserted the importance of independence was in 1882 when he tried to establish Sapporo Independent Church. Criticized by the American Methodist Foreign Mission Board, which had lent seven hundred _yen_ to them, Uchimura and his group of Christian friends returned the money in order to maintain the independence of the church. Calling the receipt for the returned money a "magna carta" for independence, Uchimura proudly wrote in italics in his diary, "S. Church is independent!" and he added, "Joy inexpressible and indescribable!"[5] This incident represented the first step in the development of Uchimura's concept of independence.

To be sure, this emphasis on independence was not confined to Uchimura alone. Among the early Christian converts were quite a few who advocated the Japanese churches' independence from foreign missions.[6] In this sense, Uchimura in this period was not very different from other Japanese Christian leaders. In fact, he attended the Second National Conference of Christians in 1883 as a delegate of the Sapporo church. The very fact that he

4. Yamamoto Taijirō,ed., _Uchimura Kanzō shinkō chosaku zenshū_ (Collected Works of Uchimura Kanzō's Religious Writings, hereafter cited as _Shinkō zenshū_), Kyōbunkan, 1963, XXIII, p. 22.

5. Zenshū, vol. 2, p. 59; and _The Complete Works of Kanzō Uchimura_ (in English), hereafter cited as _Complete Works_, with notes and comments by Yamamoto Taijirō and Mutō Yōichi, (Kyōbunkan, 1971), I, p. 86.

6. For details, see Sawa Wataru, ed., _Uemura Masahisa to sono jidai_ (Uemura Masahisa and His Times), Kyōbunkan, 1938, II, pp. 238ff.

maintained good relationships with church members and enjoyed his contact with them, however, later resulted in a strong reaction to church institutions. Reflecting on the failure of his first marriage—to a young woman he met in a church—Uchimura wrote that his religious faith at this time was nothing but a "sentimental christianity" without a real sense of sin and that church had meant merely a place to enjoy social intercourse.[7]

Despair over the failure of his marriage led Uchimura in 1884 to leave his job in the Ministry of Agriculture and travel to the United States. There, to purify himself of his sense of guilt, he threw himself into a training school for retarded children. Afterward he entered Amherst College, where he experienced his second religious conversion under the influence of President Julius H. Seelye, who made him aware of the importance of the concept of redemption. On March 8, 1886 he wrote in his diary: "In the crucifixion of the Son of God lies the solution of all the difficulties that (have) buffeted my mind thus far. Christ paying all my debts, can bring me back to the purity and innocence of the first man before the Fall."[8] Instead of relying on his own efforts as an independent fighter, he decided to depend on the Omnipotent. The awareness of his being a "child of God," despite his sinfulness, also led him to believe that even such a heathen nation as Japan could be saved by the absolute love of God.

Upon obtaining a B.S. degree from Amherst in 1887, he entered Hartford Theological Seminary, but the materialist attitudes of his fellow seminarians disappointed him. He left the Seminary and returned home in 1888 with the strong determination to fight in "the battlefield of God."[9] His mission was by this time already formulated: to serve the two J's, Jesus and Japan.

Disillusionment with the United States may be one reason why Uchimura now felt a renewed appreciation for Japan and began to see in his own country the potential for becoming a "nation of God."[10] He had gone to the United States expecting to find the "holy land." He had idealized America as a nation of Puritans. Instead, he had discovered racism and materialism. This discovery was accompanied by the awakening of a belief in God's universal desire to save all human beings and all nations. Even Japan, a nation of "heathens," thus had an opportunity to serve a Christian mission.

7. Shinkō zenshū, II, pp. 61ff.; Complete Works, I, pp. 90ff.
8. Shinkō zenshū, II, pp. 111-112; Complete Works, I, p. 153.
9. Shinkō zenshū, II, p. 159; Complete Works, I, p. 208.
10. Shinkō zenshū, II, p. 119; Complete Works, I, p. 161.

As a "most radical patriotic believer," Uchimura wanted to construct a form of Christianity that was based on a Japanese foundation. In his view, Japan's problems were due to the rapid and superficial process of westernization that had imported even Christianity simply because it was Western.[11] Consequently, when he found a teaching job in a missionary school in Niigata, he began teaching his students about such Japanese cultural traditions as Buddhism. Uchimura soon met with opposition from the missionaries, who did not approve of his nationalist views, and from fellow Japanese teachers, who fawned over the missionaries. After only three months at the school, he resigned.

Up to this point in his life, Uchimura's conflicts were primarily with American missionaries. Like many other Christian leaders in Japan, he wanted Japanese churches to be financially and administratively independent of foreign control. He also sought to create a distinctively Japanese form of Christianity. This goal was prompted in part by the general reaction to superficial westernization, but was further motivated by the need to prove that Christianity in Japan was not in conflict with kokutai, the orthodox theory of the state. The Meiji Constitution of 1889 guaranteed freedom of religion only insofar as religious belief did not interfere with the duty of subjects. Thus, it became necessary for Japanese Christians to develop a form of Christianity acceptable to the state.

Uchimura did not at first view either the Meiji Constitution or the Imperial Rescript on Education of 1890 as a threat to his freedom of religion and thought, not realizing that both would form the core of orthodox ideology. Indeed, he used the English translation of the constitution as a text for his English class in the First Higher Middle School when he started teaching there in 1890. However, the Rescript in particular soon became a symbol of Japanese morality and, ultimately, of loyalty to the emperor. Read aloud on important occasions, in a dignified ceremony conducted in every school in the country, the Rescript assumed the quality of a sacred text. Thus, in 1891, when Uchimura failed to bow low enough before the imperial signature on the Rescript, as all other students and faculty members at the school were expected to do, his seemingly disrespectful behavior created a scandal.

It is important, however, to understand the exact nature of Uchimura's transgression and the reason for it. He hesitated to perform a deep bow

11. Yamamoto Taijirō ,ed., Uchimura Kanzō nikki shokan zenshū (Diaries and Letters of Uchimura Kanzō, hereafter cited as Nikki), Kyōbunkan, 1964, V, p. 213.

before the Imperial Rescript because he was uncertain about the symbolic meaning of the ceremony: this was the first year that the ceremony was conducted, and Uchimura questioned whether the bow represented an act of emperor-worship or simply respect. If it was an act of emperor-worship, it conflicted with his Christian faith. Uchimura was aware that some Christian students who were under his influence were watching how he would behave, and, by coincidence, he happened to be reading Thomas Carlyle's biography of Oliver Cromwell, which described Cromwell's refusal to make concessions to this-worldly order.[12]

In the end, Uchimura did bow; however, he did not bow deeply. For this, he was attacked in the popular press and vilified by the mass communication media. Uchimura and his family were subjected to such extreme social pressure that he was forced to resign his teaching poisition and his wife took sick and died. Although Uchimura himself respected the content of the Rescript, others considered him disloyal to the Emperor and, in the fanatically patriotic mood of the time, he found himself to his own surprise suddenly cast as a traitor. However, this famous incident in his life and in the history of modern Japan represented not a conscious or planned defiance of political authority, but merely a mild act of noncompliance.

The lese majesty incident and Uchimura's response to it distinguished him from other nationalist Christians in Japan. Whereas they sought to reconcile the political orthodoxy of the state with Christianity, Uchimura became more defiant than ever. Other Christians, such as Yokoi Tokio or Ebina Danjō, attempted to synthesize Christian teachings with either Confucianism or Shintō.[13] In their eclectic interpretation of Christianity, they attempted to refute the argument made by Inoue Tetsujirō and others that Christianity was intrinsically incompatible with the intent of the Rescript. By contrast, Uchimura, in the face of extreme poverty and isolation, tried to find a positive meaning to the word "independence" In 1898 he founded his own magazine, entitled significantly Tokyo Dokuritsu Zasshi (Tokyo Independent Magazine), and in the following year, he attempted to explain what he meant by the term.

"Independence does not simply mean the rejection of help from outside," Uchimura wrote, "but it means making the best use of all one's abilities. Each individual is a microcosm in whom almost infinite power is reserved. If one can develop all of one's powers, one can not only realize one's

12. See Professor Ōta's essay below for Carlyle's influence on Uchimura.
13. Sawa, op. cit., I, pp. 624ff.

desires, but one can also help others. . . . Dependence is not a weakness, but a crime. Independence is not a virture; it is an imperative duty."[14] In another article written in the same year, Uchimura said, "Without fighting, no complete independence has ever been achieved."[15] Uchimura attacked every kind of dependence except for that on God. "Independence means standing directly with God and truth," he wrote. "To depend on man, on government, on temple or church, or on the company is not to be independent."[16]

Having established this principle of independence, Uchimura criticized Japanese churches for their close ties with the ruling elites. "Christianity is a religion for lower class people in particular. . . . Nevertheless, here in this country, Christians, including the late Mr. Niishima Jō and present day Christian leaders, try to please the upper class by following the example of Buddhists and Shintoists. For this very reason Christianity has become vulgarized and has lost its spirituality."[17]

The most telling example of the churches' compromise with the authorities was the Conference of Three Religions in 1912, sponsored by the Ministry of Home Affairs with the aim of "guarding and maintaining the prosperity of the Imperial Throne."[18] Many Christian leaders welcomed this conference of Christians, Buddhists, and Shintoists, believing it represented the government's recognition of Christianity as a legitimate religion. Although Uchimura himself firmly believed that "the Christianity which can save Japan should be one given birth to by the Japanese people themselves,"[19] he could not agree with many nationalist Christians who were advocating "Japanese patterns of Christianity" that made concessions to imperial orthodoxy. In a letter of September 17, 1907, to David Bell, his best friend in the United States, Uchimura complained that nationalist Christians identified Christianity with Confucianism and bushidō, and that American missionaries were tolerant enought to be sympathetic to such interpretations of Christianity. He also added that these same nationalist Christians criticized his orthodox Christian beliefs for being old-fashioned.[20]

Confronted with the compromising stand of the Japanese churches toward political authority, Uchimura concluded that the important problem

14. Shinkō zenshū, VIII, p. 64.
15. Ibid., VIII, p. 64.
16. Ibid., VIII, p. 65.
17. Ibid., XVIII, p. 63.
18. Sawa, op. cit., II, pp. 702ff.
19. Shinkō zenshū, XXIV, p. 183.
20. Nikki, VI, p. 172.

for Japanese Christians was not so much the struggle between Japanese churches and foreign missionaries, but rather the problem of church institutions per se. Thus, he decided to attack not only Christian churches in Japan, but those in the rest of the world as well. To this end, he founded a new magazine in 1901 called Mukyōkai (No-Church). In the first issue, he explained the purpose of this new publication in the following way:

> "No-Church" is a church for those who have no church. In other words, it is something like a boarding house for homeless people. It is a spiritual poorhouse or orphanage. "No" in the term "No-Church" should be understood to mean absence and not to mean "negate" or "ignore."[21]

When Uchimura proposed his idea of no-church, he still believed he was an orthodox Christian, just as, when he was accused of being a traitor to kokutai orthodoxy, he himself believed he was a genuine patriot.[22] In his view, "the highest orthodoxy is to love brethren with the heart of Christ."[23] The "most Important Heresy" was not to reject the Godness of Christ or to deny the Redemption, the Resurrection and the Assumption; rather the most important heresy was "to hate one's brethren."[24]

From 1901, the year of his publication of Mukyōkai, and especially from 1903, when he started to criticize the Russo-Japanese War, Uchimura Kanzō became a heretic in two senses: first, in relation to the imperial orthodoxy and second in relation to the Christian church. Gradually, he became aware of his status as an outcaste and even proud of it. If, at the time of the lese majesty incident in 1891, he was not ready to become a heretic, on the eve of the Russo-Japanese War, he intentionally chose to be one by firmly maintaining a pacifist stand which was extremely unpopular even among other Japanese Christians. He even cooperated with the socialists in advancing his pacifist position and when he left the Yorozu Chōhō in protest over that newspaper's pro-war stand, those who resigned with him (Kōtoku Shūsui and Sakai Toshihiko) were socialists. While he clearly distinguished his ideas from socialism in his article "Christianity and Socialism," published in 1903,[25] nevertheless he courageously associated with

21. Shinkō zenshū, XVIII, p. 86. Mukyōkai is commonly translated "Non-Church."
22. Nikki, I, p. 223. See also, Ryusaku Tsunoda, et. al., Sources of Japanese Tradition (Columbia University Press, 1958), p. 853.
23. Shinkō zenshū, VII, p. 51.
24. Ibid., VIII, p. 117.
25. Ibid., XXI, pp. 312ff.

socialists, who were already being labeled exponents of "dangerous thought." "When the truth stands by itself," he wrote, "without depending on others, people call it heresy; once the king protects it, however, people call it orthodoxy. In times of injustice, names are all reversed. I am fortunate to be hated by the 'orthodox' because I am a heretic."[26]

Uchimura eventually came to praise heresy as the vehicle of progress: "Nothing is more valuable than heresy. Without it, no progress can be expected."[27] Hence, what men should fear was not heresy, but dependence. Even so, he wrote, "there are many who fear heresy and very few who are afraid of being dependent."[28]

The First World War confirmed Uchimura in his belief of the value of no-church independence. "Once Christianity forms a church," he wrote, in an article entitled "Church and War," "it must inevitably support war. Church and the idea of war are inseparable. Once Christianity returns to its original no-church form, it will be against war. No-churchism and pacifism are inseparable."[29]

It was not simply pacifism, however, that made Uchimura a believer in no-churchism. He regarded Protestantism as "precisely dependent on nothing else but God. If we need to rely on the church, we should return to the Roman Catholic church. . . . Since the time Luther proposed freedom of belief, the church on earth has been unnecessary."[30] In 1930, Uchimura continued to believe that the "Protestant Church is a contradiction in terms."[31]

No matter how strongly Uchimura emphasized the importance of the "free independent individual," groups inevitably formed among the readers of his magazine _Seisho no Kenkyū_ (The Biblical Study) and among those who attended his weekly lectures on the Bible. He recognized the danger of the group's becoming a sort of church. "Do not talk about independence," he warned in 1913. "Talk about God. If you emphasize independence instead of God, independence will result in the establishment of a sect."[32]

26. _Ibid._, XXIII, p. 288.
27. _Ibid._, XIV, p. 220.
28. _Ibid._, VIII, p. 69.
29. _Ibid._, XXVII, pp. 83-84.
30. _Ibid._, VIII, p. 222.
31. _Ibid._, XVIII, p. 34.
32. _Ibid._, VIII, p. 67.

To prevent the creation of a sect of religious followers, Uchimura proposed forming a "spiritual group" instead of a church. The group he organized lacked a hierarchical structure and practiced no ceremonies of any sort, but insofar as it was a group of human beings with at least minimal differentiation of roles between leader and follower, it could not completely escape the tendencies which characterize any organization. Uchimura was aware of this problem, too. "Nothing is more easily corrupted than church," he remarked.[33] His solution was therefore a drastic one—a kind of permanent revolution:

> No-church should become a church. However, we should not return to a traditional church. . . . We should form a spiritual group of those who need no church. I must admit that such a group would easily become a church. In that case, we should immediately destroy it. . . . Destroy again and again, form again and again—permanently.[34]

Following his own dictum, Uchimura formed the Kashiwagi Kyōdai Dan (Kashiwagi Brethren Group) in 1918 and dissolved it three years later. Thus, Uchimura not only became a political and religious heretic, but he also became a permanent heretic.

The concept of permanent heresy was closely related to Uchimura's perception of life and institutions as being antithetical. "Life is more valuable than institutions. Life does not work according to rules. . . . Life works by itself and not as a group." The organization of individuals into institutions involved the loss of the individual's independence; "Belief should be independent, whereas institutions mean dependence."[35] Hence, true religious belief, Uchimura seemed to imply, required the destruction of institutions. In this sense, Uchimura's ideas resembled anarchism.

The need to destroy institutions involved more than the problem of the church: Uchimura applied this idea to all secular institutions, in particular, political ones. His cynicism also extended to ideologies, including liberalism and democracy. He characterized Japanese society as "the society in which isms are easily corrupted. . . . In Japan, no matter how sacred the principle, it cannot maintain its dignity for more than three years."[36] Uchimura's

33. Ibid., VI, p. 198.
34. Ibid., XVIII, p. 102.
35. Ibid., XVIII, p. 89.
36. Ibid., XXIV, p. 132.

skepticism of politicians was total: "Despise politics," he warned in 1902. "Then you will be able to reform it. . . . Politicians are like servants, aren't they? . . . Nevertheless, people look up to them by making them men of rank. Aren't they respecting servants as masters?"[37]

This keen distrust of politics and politicians did not mean that Uchimura was a populist. If he had no faith in the ruling elites, he also placed little trust in the masses. Earlier in his life he had thought that corruption in Japanese society was limited to the upper stratum, but gradually he became pessimistic about Japanese society in general. "There is no public opinion in Japan," he wrote in 1924. "Nor can we stir up public opinion. There is a deep-seated reason for this. The Japanese people have not discovered individuality. People who lack self-awareness cannot have any decisive opinions. So-called public opinion is nothing but blind following."[38] Disenchanted with democratic goals, Uchimura concluded that, "In this world, majority always means vulgar. Therefore, one who is proud of being in the majority is simply demonstrating his own vulgarity."[39] Elsewhere, he wrote caustically, "American missionaries taught us many cursed errors. The most serious of these is trust in the majority, based on their false idea of democracy."[40]

Coupled with Uchimura's sense of the hopelessness of the domestic political situation was his despair over international events. America's entrance into World War I shattered his last remaining sense of optimism; he had expected the United States to serve as a mediator for peace and now, in 1918, with all hope gone, Uchimura began talking about the Second Coming of Christ. The Great Tokyo Earthquake of 1923 deepened his gloom: he felt as though the earthquake was God's judgment.[41] Living in seclusion in a house in Kashiwagi, which he jokingly referred to as the "Temple of Prophecy,"[42] he avoided going to downtown Tokyo—the "city of Babylon."

During these postwar years, Uchimura continued to publish The Biblical Study and to give a talk on the Bible every Sunday. But although in his later years he was often called the "Saint of Kashiwagi," the twilight of his life was not tranquil. The militancy of his religious belief would not allow him tranquility. "Christianity is not religion to lead you to peace of mind," he wrote

37. Ibid., XXI, p. 213.
38. Ibid., XIV, p. 301.
39. Ibid., XVIII, p. 222.
40. Ibid., XVIII, p. 199.
41. Nikki, II, p. 350.
42. Ibid., III, p. 227.

in 1925. "It is a way of fighting against this world and gaining a victory over it. . . . If you want peace of mind, you should rely on Buddhism instead. . . . Christianity confronts this world, fights against it, and conquers it under the Justice of God. Therefore, hard battle is inevitable."[43]

The one battle he fought to his dying day was the battle against institutionalized religion. Here, too, as in so many of his other struggles, his efforts were in vain, for although he prized independence more than any other principle, he could not prevent his followers from violating or misconstruing the meaning of that word. In 1930, the year of his death, he reiterated his belief that independence was evidence of true faith:

> Independence is different from isolation. Independence means standing with God, whereas isolation means inability to stand with anything. . . . Independent people love other independent people. When independent people unite with each other, the strongest group can be realized.[44]

If independence is understood as being with God, and if God is for everyone, then, theoretically all human beings can be united. "The positive aspects of no-churchism," he wrote in his diary on October 2, 1929, "should be the idea of a church which includes all human beings."[45]

Yet, in practice, there was disunity and disagreement among members of the no-church group. Only a month earlier, Uchimura had written in his diary, "Now the no-church group is becoming a church. Quite a few so-called no-churchists are not only criticizing the churches, but they are also criticizing each other. They are saying, 'We are the genuine no-churchists.' In so saying, some of them are even proud to criticize Mr. Uchimura, who is the founder of no-churchism."[46] Soon after, he confided in his diary that "No-churchism is a principle which cannot be realized in this world. . . . The real value of no-churchism lies in the impossibility of its realization."[47] Pursuing this impossibility, Uchimura died less than a half year later, on March 28, 1930.

How can we locate Uchimura Kanzō within the context of modern Japanese intellectual history in general and within the framework of orthodox

43. Shinkō zenshū, XVIII, p. 185.
44. Ibid., XVIII, p. 35.
45. Nikki, IV, p. 352.
46. Ibid., IV, p. 350.
47. Ibid., IV, p. 358.

and heterodox thought in particular? Uchimura's emphasis on independence recalls the teaching of another great Japanese thinker, Fukuzawa Yukichi. Both men emphasized the importance of the independence of the nation as well as that of the individual and both saw a close relationship between the two. However, in Fukuzawa's optimistic outlook, there was no necessary conflict between the independence of the individual and the independence of the nation, though in his later years he tended to emphasize the latter. In Uchimura's case, on the other hand, only an ideal nation could coexist with independent individuals: the existing nation-state was the enemy of individual independence. Moreover, in Uchimura's later years, he increasingly stressed the importance of individual independence.

This difference between Uchimura and Fukuzawa may be due, at least in part, to the differences in their personality and termperament. Fukuzawa was optimistic and secular, while Uchimura was pessimistic and religious. A more salient difference, however, is generational.

For Fukuzawa, who experienced the Meiji Restoration around the middle of his life, the most important task was to overcome feudal society and to establish a modern nation-state. For Uchimura, who was only seven years old at the time of the Restoration, the nation-state was already a given fact. What he confronted in his early adulthood was first, imperial orthodoxy, and second, Japan's rapid and unbalanced development. The spiritual and material problems created by what Natsume Sōseki called "development impelled from without" were difficulties that Fukuzawa never seriously experienced or even anticipated.

There is no doubt that Uchimura was sensitive to the problems of the time and fought fiercely against social evils in his own way. The question remains, how effective were his efforts? One may criticize his "retreatist" and "apolitical" attitudes for their ineffectiveness in changing the social situation. We should be careful, however, not to expect what we cannot and should not expect of him. He defined his role, or his mission—to use his favorite word—as that of heresy or dissent. He did not wish to be in the majority. Therefore, when we evaluate his role in Japanese history, we should first of all examine whether he was successful in playing his part as a dissenting minority. At the end of his life, on the eve of the militarist era, he became a prophet of the fall of the nation. One of his disciples, Tokyo Imperial University Professor Yanaibara Tadao, following in his footsteps, also prophesized the defeat of the Japanese empire and resisted imperialist war. As a consequence, like Uchimura, he lost his job. If we consider that, except for those communists who refused to recant, very few Japanese resisted imperialism in Japan, then we must admit that Uchimura and the no-church Christians played an important role as political dissenters.

One may raise the further question of why no-church Christians could not become a majority at this time, even though their pacifist views were later proved correct. Here we see the dilemma of dissenters. If they try to play a role as a genuine political minority, they must remain in the minority; but if they want to be influential, they must become a majority. In fact, this is the dilemma characterized by Ernst Troeltsch as "sect-type" group versus "church type" group. The sect-type group cannot become a huge organization, but nevertheless can play an important role in revitalizing the larger and more influential established organization.[48] Is it possible to retain one's dissenting opinion while at the same time exerting influence on a large scale? Uchimura's troubled life casts new light on this knotty problem.

48. Ernst Troeltsch, Die Soziallehren der Christliche Kirchen und Gruppen (J.C. B. Mohr, 1912).

# UCHIMURA KANZŌ AT AMHERST

Ōyama Tsunao
and
Ray A. Moore

Uchimura Kanzō's attitude toward America often swung wildly between adulation and extreme criticism. Yet he cherished his relationship with at least two Americans all of his life: Julius H. Seelye, the fourth president of Amherst College, under whom he studied from 1885 to 1887; and David C. Bell, whom he met first in Washington, D.C., in 1884 and corresponded with frequently until the end of his life. His respect for these two men did not falter even when he became most critical of American policy during the debate over the 1924 Exclusion Act, and it was partly because of them that he was able to return eventually to a balanced judgment of the United States. For Uchimura, good Christian America was represented by people like Seelye and Bell.

One key to understanding Uchimura's attitude toward America lies in his relationship with Julius Seelye during his stay at Amherst, where he found his Christian identity and formed a favorable image of Christian America.

Uchimura once wrote: "To be sure, my Christian faith comes from New England, the home of Puritanism."[1] Not only had Amherst College in western Massachusetts produced his two Christian mentors—William S. Clark, the founder of Sapporo Agricultural College, Uchimura's alma mater in Hokkaido; and Julius Seelye—but also it played a significant role in his own life. Admitted to the junior class as a special student in his mid-twenties, Uchimura experienced conversion to true Christian redemption under the tutelage of Seelye. He also studied history under Anson D. Morse, and it was this experience that later strengthened his Christian view of history.

1. Yamamoto Taijirō, ed., Uchimura Kanzō shinkō chosaku zenshū (Collected Works of Uchimura Kanzō's Religious Writings, hereafter referred to as Shinkō zenshū), XXIII (Kyōbunkan, 1963), p. 118.

Meanwhile, he continued to struggle for a resolution to the problem of the contradiction which he saw between the Bible and natural science. Indeed, his stay at Amherst represents his "moratorium" in the long process by which he was transformed into an evangelical and militant Christian.

Amherst was not the destination Uchimura had in mind when he thought of coming to America, although he had known of its existence through his American teachers and through books he had read in Sapporo. When Uchimura sailed for American in 1884, after the failure of his first marriage, he possessed a vague notion of dedicating his life to the service of humanity through philanthropic work. But after half a year of hard work with mentally retarded children in Elwyn, Pennsylvania, he collapsed physically and mentally. At this point, Niishima Jō, who was paying his second visit to America, learned of Uchimura's deep depression through Ōta (later Nitobe) Inazō, Uchimura's old friend from Sapporo who was then studying at Johns Hopkins University. It was Niishima who suggested that Uchimura go to Amherst. Niishima, a graduate of Amherst in the class of 1870, had a special agreement with Seelye whereby Amherst would accept up to six Japanese students on his recommendation.[2] Meanwhile, Uchimura received an offer of financial aid from other sources to study medicine at the University of Pennsylvania, or to attend Harvard University. After a long, serious deliberation during the summer of 1885, he chose Amherst, because, he wrote, Seelye's writings attracted him, and because "Amherst esteems virtue not knowledge; principles not enterprise; spiritual training; and not mere encyclopedic breadth. She urges her students to communicate with Nature and Nature's God and makes of them creative minds independent of the succor of Authority."[3]

He believed he had made the right choice. In later years he fondly recalled his days at Amherst and even tended to idealize the college:

> I have come to realize the true value of the pursuit of learning through a college education, where learning was introduced to me not merely as a financial venture, but as a spiritually and emotionally noble enterprise.[4]

2. Otis Cary, "Uchimura, Neesima, and Amherst—Recently Discovered Correspondence", in Japan Quarterly (October-December, 1956) Vol. IV, pp.XXX-XXX.
3. Zenshū Vol. 2 (1962), pp. 211-212.
4. Ibid., p. 228.

On another occasion he wrote:

> I understand the spirit of my college to be noble independence, brave defiance of hollow shows of all kinds, patient and reverential search after Truth, orthodoxy in the anti-head religion sense of the term.[5]

Uchimura was not satisfied with the college in terms of his own intellectual achievement, however. Had he wished to obtain further intellectual stimulation or practical skills, he might have gone to Harvard, as he admits, or might have chosen Pennsylvania. He had already earned a B.S. degree from Sapporo Agricultural College before coming to America. Had he gone to Harvard or Pennsylvania, surely he would not have lamented, "As for my intellectual gains in my college, they amounted to but very little."[6] He could have gone to such American institutions as his friends of the "Sapporo Band"—Miyabe Kingō went to Harvard, Ōta Inazō and Satō Shōsuke to Johns Hopkins University. But it is significant that Uchimura dared to choose Amherst while only vaguely perceiving the difference between a college and a university. He seems to have known that it was a college that he needed, and this was an indication of his strong need to seek direction and purpose in his life. Compared to his close friends at Harvard and Johns Hopkins, who had been promised professorships at their alma mater on completion of their graduate studies in America, he alone was drifting in a sea of continual depression. He had graduated _summa cum laude_ from Sapporo, but relatively minor job opportunities had been offered to him. What Uchimura needed to do in the summer of 1885 was to find himself and make a decision on the direction of his life. Niishima's advice probably played a major role in steering Uchimura's life in the direction that he had felt ought to be his own. Seelye's Amherst seemed to Uchimura to be the place where his vague intention to become a Christian worker might be clarified and the purpose of his life determined.

Seelye's presence there was a major factor in attracting Uchimura to Amherst. At his first meeting with Seelye, Uchimura was deeply impressed with "a large well-built figure, the leonine eyes suffused with tears, the warm grasp of hands unusually tight, orderly words of welcome and sympathy. . . I

5. _Ibid._, p. 124; and _The Complete Works of Kanzō Uchimura_ (in English, Kyōbunkan, 1971-72); hereafter referred to as _Complete Works_, with Notes and Comments by Yamamoto Taijirō and Mutō Yōichi, Vol. 1, p. 167.
6. _Zenshū_, Vol. 2, p. 124; _Complete Works_, Vol. 1, pp. 166-167.

at once felt a peculiar ease in myself. I confided myself to his help which he most gladly promised."[7] As a matter of fact, Uchimura's idealistic image of Seelye had been formed well before their first meeting. While still in Japan, he had read Seelye's proposal for the renovation of Japanese education, contained in Seelye's letter to Mori Arinori in 1872, as well as his criticism of Darwinism. Seelye's image as a Christian educator and thinker became more solidified, and idealized, after the initial meeting in Amherst in 1885.

Although apparently unknown to Uchimura, Seelye had had by 1885 more than fifteen years of contact with Japan, first as one of Niishima's teachers from 1867 to 1870, second through a one-month visit to Japan in 1872, and third as a kind of unofficial advisor through correspondence with Tanaka Fujimaro, Vice-Minister of Education, during the 1870s and 1880s. The presence of Niishima at Amherst during the Meiji Restoration and the early days of the new era aroused Seelye's interest in the opening of Japan and the ensuing turmoil that led to the demise of the Tokugawa regime. He was surprisingly well informed about Japan, having read much of the literature then available. His opportunity to express his views on the future of Japan came in 1872 when Mori Arinori sent a set of questions to leading American educators, including President Stearns and Professor Seelye of Amherst, regarding the influence of education on a nation's development. Although Seelye was quick to respond to the questions, he could suggest little more than "instruction of the true religion" as the means of strengthening the nation.[8] Later that year Mori and Tanaka Fujimaro visited Amherst and observed at first-hand the evangelical Christian belief that the development of character through religious training was the prime objective of education. It was during this visit in the spring of 1872 that Seelye's interest in Japan quickened and he conceived the idea of traveling there. He had long contemplated a trip around the world, and Tanaka's invitation to Japan seems to have been a major impetus in his departure in the summer of 1872.[9]

Accompanied by his friend, Edward Hitchcock, the college physician and director of physical education, and the son of a famous geologist and former president of Amherst, Seelye visited in August and September 1872 Yokohama, "Yeddo" (Tokyo), the new port of Kobe and several other ports in the Inland Sea. His reputation as an educator and his letter on the subject to

7. Zenshū, Vol. 2, p. 105; Complete Works, Vol. 1, p. 145.
8. Ivan Hall, Mori Arinori (Cambridge: Harvard University Press, 1973), p. 183.
9. "Trip to Japan, China and India," in Julius H. Seelye Papers, Amherst College Archives.

Mori Arinori earlier in the year had marked him in the minds of Meiji leaders as a visiting dignitary. He dined at the imperial palace with the Meiji Emperor and principal leaders, again presented his views on education, discussed with Ōki Takatō the possible use of the Shimonoseki indemnity for purposes of education, and (he proudly recorded in his diary) preached the first Christian sermon in Tokyo after the government lifted its ban. In side trips to Kamakura and Enoshima, Seelye and Hitchcock viewed the Kamakura Daibutsu and gathered rock specimens for Amherst's famous collection. Seelye also met the elderly father of Niishima Jō, his first Japanese student, and in Kobe had a stiff encounter with the governor of Hyōgo prefecture and the father of another Japanese student who had arrived in Amherst in 1872, Kanda Naibu. Though Seelye's visit to Japan, and later to China and India, was brief, it was the beginning of several years of contact with Tanaka Fujimaro and other Japanese concerning problems of Japanese education. In 1873 and 1874 Tanaka wrote to Seelye of the new Kaisei gakkō established by the government, and mentioned with pride the new normal schools and foreign language schools. Seelye informed Tanaka of his own involvement in the public campaign to persuade the American Congress, in which he served one term in 1874-76, to use the Shimonoseki indemnity to support education abroad for young Japanese.

In 1876, while he was Vice-Minister of Education and charged with instituting a system of physical education in the schools, Tanaka again visited Amherst to consult with the new president, Julius Seelye, and to observe the college's remarkable system of physical education and gymnastic exercises, which had already captivated several Japanese. Indian clubs, wooden dumbbells, rings, and wands—all moved in precise military fashion under the direction of a drill instructor and accompanied by piano music. So famous were Dr. Edward Hitchcock's gymnastic exercises that some 6,000 visitors flocked to Barrett Hall to observe the physical education classes in the 1876-77 academic year! Much impressed by what he saw, Tanaka later wrote to Seelye requesting his assistance in securing the services of "an experienced and skilled instructor in gymnastics to. . . teach the exercises to male and female students of our schools. . . ."[10] Seelye's choice was George A. Leland, class of 1874 and captain of the gymnastics team for four years, who had just finished Harvard Medical School and his internship when the Meiji government's offer came. Other contacts between Seelye and Tanaka continued through the early 1880s.

10. Letter from Tanaka to Seelye, March 6, 1878, in Seelye Papers, Amherst College Archives.

Although he never had the strong influence of a David Murray on Japanese education in the 1870s, Seelye did forge the first link between Amherst and Japan through his sponsorship and tutelage of Niishima, Kanda, Uchimura and other young Japanese students; and his association with Tanaka Fujimaro. These years of concern for Japan lay behind his decision to admit Uchimura to the college and the warmth with which he greeted him in the summer of 1885. Niishima's agreement with Seelye enabled Uchimura to stay at Amherst without the burden of tuition and board. He thus started his second college life in September 1885 with a spiritual ease and with little need to concern himself about his material well-being.

With his background in the natural sciences, Uchimura earned good marks in both geology and mineralogy, but courses in inductive reasoning proved troublesome for him.[11] Being a foreigner and several years older than most of the other students, he seems to have found it difficult to make friends. Indeed, he seldom referred to friends' names when he recalled Amherst in later years. Although it is known only through anecdote, Uchimura was involved in one extra-curricular activity, i.e., he was a member of the "Hitchcock Society of Inquiry," in which he seems to have tried to develop his debating skills.[12] Otherwise he remained rather aloof from student life. His concentration on Biblical study two hours a day looked, he felt, rather strange and peculiar to others.[13] Observing his earnest attitude toward Biblical and evangelical studies, his fellow students invented an adjective, "Uchimural," which perhaps referred to Uchimura's aloofness from the student body and, at the same time, his stalwart devotion to the college's inner goals.[14] He struck most students as a bit peculiar. In spite of the poor grades he received in Seelye's own classes in Moral Philosophy and Catechism, he remained one of Seelye's most earnest students.

Due to his strong spiritual attachment to Seelye, Uchimura depicted Amherst idealistically. The college's place in the changing situation of American higher education in the 1880's and the question of how Seelye was to adjust to it were matters that lay beyond Uchimura's perview. Uchimura praised very highly, for instance, the elective system of courses which he called optional studies:

11. School Record 408, Special, Class of 1887, Uchimura, Jon Kanzō of Sapporo, Japan, Original in Amherst College Archives.
12. Amherst College Olio '87, p. 65; and Amherst College Olio '88, p. 65.
13. Zenshū, Vol. 13, p. 23.
14. Amherst College Olio '88, p. 12.

> Optional studies enlarge the area where each student can discover and refine his own talents. . . Indeed the College indicates the divine calling for each and every student. . . Optional studies extend to the College the character of a university.[15]

He also believed that the college developed the so-called "scholar" who, in Emerson's terminology, loves the truth for its own sake.[16]

But he failed to realize that the idea of "extending to the College the character of a university" or "the truth for its own sake" had not been the traditional aim of Amherst and other New England colleges. Rather, these were challenging new trends. He failed to see that New England colleges were being thrown into turmoil over how to encounter and adjust to, or overcome, the wave of these new ideas and the university movement that spread out from such big universities as Harvard and Johns Hopkins.[17]

Seelye's Amherst was in fact passing through this period of unsettling change during Uchimura's two years on campus from 1885 to 1887. In the social and cultural changes of the late nineteenth century, New England church-related private colleges struggled to achieve a synthesis between the changing American culture and the expectations of New England conservatism. How was the college to respond to the challenge issued by Noah Webster at the opening of Amherst in 1830 "to check the progress of errors which are propagated from Cambridge"?[18] This had been the central task of Amherst presidents ever since. A highly qualified leader was needed in the 1880's in the face of the university movement. Harvard's new orientation, steered by Charles Eliot, and the establishment of Johns Hopkins in 1876 began to exert influence upon all American higher education. Harvard's and Johns Hopkins's concept of the university, which had been inherited from Germany, advocated academic freedom, truth for its own sake, and an objective methodology of learning. It stressed a specialized curriculum based upon electives rather than liberal arts composed of required courses. In addition,

15. Zenshū, Vol. 2, p. 217.
16. Ibid., p. 228.
17. On the university movement, see Richard Hofstadter and Walter P. Meger, The Development of Academic Freedom in the United States, (New York, 1955); and Richard Hofstadter and Wilson Smith, eds., American Higher Education, (Chicago, 1961), Vols. 1 and 2. As for the tension between the New England colleges and the university movement, see George E. Peterson, The New England College in the Age of the University, (Amherst, 1964).
18. Letter from Noah Webster to William Leffingwell, Sept. 27, 1820. Manuscript in Amherst College Archives.

strong voices arose in the western part of the country criticizing the paternalistic and aristocratic character of private colleges in New England, and calling for the formation of state universities.

In the late 1860s, following the moral crusade of the Civil War, Amherst had undergone a great revival. Amherst faculty and students believed fervently that education must mean Christian education, and that Amherst must be an evangelical Christian school. This spirit was expressed by Julius Seelye when he wrote: "Unless we make Christian culture the informing idea of all our educational edifice, unless we make the Bible its cornerstone and top stone, the edifice itself will crumble."[19] For New England conservatives, the ideal scholar was not a specialist who adhered to liberal thinking but one who had achieved a balance between religion and intellectual pursuits and who lived a life of harmony in the Biblical sense. This image of the "whole man" was what Seelye's predecessors at Amherst had sought after.[20] The development of character had been, and would remain under Seelye, the primary objective of the college. As President Stearns had declared in 1872, character was of greater consequence than intellect, being "chiefly made up of moral principles, right purposes, appropriate emotions and practical wisdom."[21] To pray well had been considered to study well; and the peril to the college, they believed, had been the inclination to place scholarship ahead of piety.[22] It was in keeping with this tradition that Seelye was chosen president in 1876. The responsibility placed on his shoulders was heavy indeed.

At Seelye's inauguration, Roswell D. Hitchcock, representing the Board of Trustees, referred to the urgent conflict between religion and science and the wave of the university movement, and stated the Trustees' charge to Seelye: "We shall send you raw boys, to be sent back to us accomplished Christian scholars and gentlemen."[23] Responding to Hitchcock, Seelye declared his resolve to maintain Amherst as a Christian institution. Aware of the Spencerian view of civilization, he declared:

19. Thomas Le Duc, Piety and Intellect at Amherst College, 1865-1912 (New York, 1946), p. 23.
20. George E. Peterson, The New England College, p. 27ff.
21. Le Duc, Piety and Intellect, p. 26.
22. Ibid., p. 22.
23. Addresses at the Inauguration of Rev. Julius H. Seelye (Springfield, 1877), p. 8.

> It will help us to a clear view and correct conclusion, if we divest ourselves at the outset of the very common but quite superficial notion that there is an inherent law of progress in human nature, by which it is constantly seeking and gaining for itself an imposed condition. Such a notion is not supported by the facts either of history or of human nature itself. The facts of history certainly show a far more prominent law of deterioration than of progress.[24]

And human progress, according to Seelye, was not made by man, "but by the simple preaching of the gospel, by the story of God's grace, which makes a man feel that he is a sinner, and gives him first longing for a better state."[25]

For Seelye, the raison d'etre of an educational institution was to make students aware of the law of deterioration and make them look upward. In his guidance of students Seelye, like his predecessors, maintained the principle, "Give them the light first."[26] This was the Seelye that Uchimura, and Niishima before him, had idealized. This was the man whose forceful defense of religion against Spencer's view of history and defense of religion as the central purpose of education had attracted Uchimura to Amherst in 1885. And yet Seelye was no antediluvian defender of the status quo in education. Having studied in Germany, he was fully conscious of the changing academic situation there and of the merits of German academism. It is not entirely surprising, then, that rather than stand unbending against the rising tide, Seelye chose the way of compromise. In contrast to other New England colleges' stubborn rejection of the elective system, Amherst increased elective courses in Seelye's second year.[27]

But how could the give-them-light-first principle coexist with a liberal elective system? Without the resolution of this question, Amherst might have lost its identity as a New England Christian college. Perhaps it was for this purpose that Seelye conducted a seminar required of all seniors, which he called "Catechism." Uchimura, who took the course during his second year at Amherst, wrote that it was "one of the courses which merited my special attention."[28]

24. Ibid., p. 15.
25. Ibid., p. 23.
26. Le Duc, Piety and Intellect, p. 56.
27. Catalogue of Amherst College for the Year 1877-1878.
28. Zenshū, Vol. 2, p. 227.

In this course students were encouraged to submit any questions relating to the whole area of learning, either taught in the college thus far or not, and Seelye answered each question. It was in this course that Seelye attempted to synthesize the expectations of New England conservatism and a liberal arts program substantially composed of elective courses. The Catechism class was the finishing touch to the Amherst education; it was also an expression of Seelye's responsibility as a Christian educator to New England conservatism.

The accomplishment of this task seems to have been possible in part because of Seelye's personal charisma. Some classes were no different from those of a university, but the college's traditional identity became apparent when the whole college gathered at the chapel to worship God under the leadership of President Seelye. Uchimura shared the feeling of others at Amherst that "it was enough that he (Seelye) stood up in the chapel, gave out a hymn, read from the Scripture and prayed."[29]

Although Niishima—who had studied at Amherst in the late 1860's when the institution was most typically Congregational—recommended that Uchimura go to Amherst, he does not seem to have perceived Amherst's dilemma in the 1880's. But Niishima trusted in Seelye's personal power as an evangelical Christian educator; and Niishima's judgment was right. Seelye's excellence as an educator and administrator is exceedingly clear when he is compared with his successor, Merrill Gates, whose evangelistic spirit lacked an appreciation for the new status of learning in the United States. Under Gates, the college almost lost the essential qualities of an institution of higher education.[30]

Turning for a moment to the whole question of the structural shift of higher education in America, one sees that Seelye belonged to the last generation of educators in New England colleges who put more emphasis on evangelism than rationalism. In this sense Uchimura belonged to the last generation of students to study under Seelye's paternalistic discipline. Three years after Uchimura graduated Seelye resigned, in 1890, because of failing health.

Any account of Uchimura's years at Amherst must include an evaluation of Seelye's influence on his development as a Christian. As is well known, Uchimura was converted to Christianity in the evangelistic

29. Ibid., p. 108; Complete Works, Vol. 1, p. 148.
30. Le Duc, Piety and Intellect, p. 135ff.

atmosphere created at Sapporo by W. S. Clark and was baptized by an American Methodist missionary. However, it is only with considerable caution that one can define this experience as true conversion to Christianity. Yet it is certain that through his Sapporo experience he was liberated from contradictory commandments of the polytheistic religion of Shintoism. What he discovered in reading the Bible and in listening to the preaching of the senior students was the existence of one God who orders an ethical way of life for mankind. It was the God of the Judaic tradition, and apparently nothing more than that. Uchimura seems to have understood intellectually the meaning of the coming of Jesus, his sufferings, the Crucifixion and the Resurrection, but it was not until he had spent his first winter in Amherst that he achieved a personal faith in the Christian concept of redemption.

One day Seelye gave Uchimura this advice:

> You shouldn't be confined and look only within yourself. Look up and outward. Stop self-reflection and turn your eyes up to Jesus who redeemed your sins on the Cross.[31]

Uchimura could appreciate Seelye's meaning intellectually, but he had yet to experience it as a reality. Noteworthy in his religious development is the fact that a "monastic life" in Amherst drove him to deeper self-reflection and made him hope for a solid Christian faith. In his late adolescence he had spent many solitary days in deliberation and self-reflection. He continued to suffer from depression in mounting intensity after his arrival in the United States, and he continued to pray for relief from it. It was in such a state of groping for help that Seelye's advice was given him. One day near the end of the first winter, Uchimura grasped experientially what Seelye meant. On March 8, 1886, he wrote in his diary:

> March 8 — Very important day in my life. Never was the atoning power of Christ more clearly revealed to me than it is today. In the crucifixion of the Son of God lies the soluion of all the difficulties that buffeted my mind thus far. Christ, paying all my debts, can bring me back to the purity and innocence of the first man before the Fall. Now I am God's child, and my duty is to believe Jesus. For His sake, God will give me all I want. He will use me for His glory, and will save me in Heaven at last.[32]

31. Zenshū, Vol. 23, p. 119.
32. Zenshū, Vol. 2, p. 111; Complete Works, Vol. 1, p. 153.

Thus, after careful tutelage, Seelye had been able to "give" Uchimura "the light first."

On the day after this spiritual experience, William S. Clark, Uchimura's other mentor, died at Amherst. Uchimura learned from the pastor who was with Clark at his death that he had cherished his eight months of Christian work in Sapporo as the most important and proudest time of his life. Soon Uchimura sent the Christian Union (later Outlook) a long eulogy applauding layman Clark's missionary work in Japan.[33] There had been no one among the members of the Sapporo Band who had decided to dedicate himslf to be what Clark cherished most--a worker for Jesus. But now under the influence of Seelye's counsel and the shock of Clark's death, Uchimura reached a new determination to be a Christian worker in Japan. Over the horizon a new outlook for the future was appearing--to live for Jesus and Japan. Toward the end of the senior year, he wrote in a letter to Seelye:

> As my time in college draws near its close my heart is filled with gratitude when I remember in what condition, physical and spiritual, I came to Amherst, and in what condition I am going to leave it. Allow me to confess, dear President, that I am one of those blessed few of my countrymen whom the Lord hath quickened through you, and who can never forget to praise Him as often as they remember you.[34]

He quietly decided to go to the Hartford Theological Seminary to further his study of Christianity.

In the years 1885-87 Amherst was being forced by outside pressure to change. Nevertheless the old Amherst remained alive as long as Seelye was its President. Amherst under Seelye was a refuge for the old New England values.[35] At the same time, it maintained its institutional identity as a college which provided a respite from the cares of the world for young men to find their respective callings in life. What Uchimura had needed was a place

33. The Christian Union, April 22, 1886, p. 7ff.
34. Letter from Uchimura to Seelye, June 17, 1887. Manuscript in Amherst College Archives.
35. For example, a writer to The Congregationalist, Sept. 14, 1881, wrote as follows: "The patrons of the College (Amherst) have sent their sons there not because they supposed it would give them a higher mental training than Harvard or Yale would, but because they believed the moral atmosphere of the College was more bracing and wholesome, and their sons could breathe it more safely."

where he could explore and clarify his still vague intentions about life, not a place where specialization was stressed prior to finding one's self. He was far behind his classmates at Sapporo in deciding the course of his life. His second turn at college life--a kind of detour--was the only road for him to tread, even though it took two more years from his life. At Amherst, which he characterized as an institution that "keeps gradualism avoiding a dash,"[36] Uchimura caught a glimpse of his life's destiny.

He never felt, however, that he had become a "whole man" while at Amherst. Several important questions were left unanswered. Seelye's pessimistic view of history, based on the belief of human deterioration, did not necessarily persuade Uchimura, because he had also studied under the historian A. D. Morse, whose lectures were colored with a belief in human progress.[37] Nor had Uchimura been able to resolve through discussion in his geology class or elsewhere his doubts about the theory of evolution. That subject was allowed to be taken up only in Seelye's classes, where Darwinian theory was rejected as groundless speculation.[38] Even so, Seelye was a "whole man" in a passing generation. Uchimura felt that as Seelye held both a Doctor of Divinity and a Doctor of Philosophy degree, he was a truly well-rounded Christian of great intellectual powers. He was the man who could respond to students' questions and doubts in the light of the Bible without compromising his Christian principles. In his search for the image of the "whole man" as conceived by Seelye, Uchimura would have to struggle with the question of the meaning of history and nature in a new generation. But at least Seelye and Amherst had armed him with a solid traditional Christian faith with which to carry on the struggle. In later years Uchimura came to believe that the concept of progress in natural history ought to be reinterpreted in the light of the Providence which he believed leads nature and history.[39] Before him, however, lay a long, toilsome journey.

36. Zenshū, Vol. 2, p. 211.
37. Ibid., pp. 218-19.
38. The Independent, Dec. 18, 1879; and The Observer, Dec. 11 and Dec. 24, 1879; and Jan. 8, 1880.
39. Matsuzawa Hiroaki, "Uchimura Kanzō no Rekishi Ishiki," in Hokudai Hōgaku Ronshū, Vol. XVII, No. 4 (1967); Vol XVIII, No. 1 (1967); and Vol. XIX, No. 4 (1968).

# UCHIMURA KANZŌ AND AMERICA: SOME REFLECTIONS ON THE PSYCHOLOGICAL STRUCTURE OF ANTI-AMERICANISM

Hirakawa Sukehiro

Just as a man like Mori Ōgai cannot be omitted from discussion of Japanese-European relations, so Uchimura Kanzō is one figure not to be neglected when relations between Japan and America are discussed. Mori Ōgai did not exhibit any extreme reaction toward Japan's relationship with the west, but Uchimura Kanzō's response was so strong that in 1924 he was referred to as a "champion of the 'hate-America' movement."[1] To a great extent, Uchimura's attitude was an outgrowth of his own problematic personality. But that it also owed something to his being a Christian should not be discounted. His value system had roots outside Japan, and America held a large part of his heart; when he asserted himself as a Japanese, it seems he could not help becoming emphatically anti-American. Throughout his life, he continued to have ambivalent and seemingly contradictory feelings toward the United States.

The eldest son of a samurai household of the Takasaki-han, Uchimura Kanzō was a patriotic man of Meiji, with memories of being exposed to the menacing strengths of western nations. At the same time, he was a Christian, a man who during his early adulthood spend nearly four years in the United States. He thus could be very sensitive to problems in Japanese-American

The original Japanese is from my Seiō no shōgeki to Nihon (The Impact of the West and Japan), pp. 161-199, vol. VI of Jinrui bunka shi (The Cultural History of Mankind), Kōdansha, 1974. I wish to thank John Boccellari, Tsukuba University, for the English translation.

1. For the strong reaction of Uchimura to the Immigration Act of 1924, see Ota Yūzō, Uchimura Kanzō: sono sekaishugi to Nihonshugi o megutte (World and Nation in Modern Japanese Christianity: The Case of Uchimura Kanzō), Kenkyūsha, 1977, pp. 227-257.

relations. Uchimura expressed his sentiments quite vividly in How I Became a Christian,[2] a work he wrote in English for American readers. I would here like to examine its sixth chapter, "The First Impressions of Christendom."

Right after his divorce from his first wife in 1884 he set out almost compulsively for America. Uchimura tells of his first impression of America, his "Holy Land," as follows:

> At the day-break of Nov. 24, 1884, my enraptured eyes first caught the faint views of Christendom. Once more I descended to my steerage-cabin, and there I was upon my knees;--the moment was too serious for me to join with the popular excitement of the hour. As the low Coast Range came clearer to my views, the sense of my dreams being now realized overwhelmed me with gratitude, and tears trickled rapidly down my cheeks. Soon the Golden Gate was passed, and all the chimneys and mast-tops now presented to my vision appeared like so many church-spires pointing toward the sky. . . . As my previous acquaintance with the Caucasian race had been mostly with missionaries, the idea stuck close to my mind; and so all the people whom I met in the street appeared to me like so many ministers fraught with high Christian purpose, and I could not but imagine myself as walking among the congregation of the First-born.

Twenty-three years old at the time, he had "learnt all that was noble, useful, and uplifting through the vehicle of the English language," starting with the Bible and biblical commentaries. Then too, the "great men" he had learned about, George Washington and the like, were for the most part Americans or Englishmen. He writes of these ideals in a rather poetic vein.

> My idea of Christian America was lofty, religious, Puritanic. I dreamed of its templed hills, and rocks that rang with hymns and praises. Hebraisms, I thought, to be the prevailing speech of the American commonality, and cherub and cherubim, hallelujahs and amens, the common language of its streets.

As Uchimura entered into conversation with people he encountered on the streets, this sort of vision quickly crumbled away. Living in straitened circumstances, confronted by the difference of customs, and above all

2. How I Became a Christian. Reprinted by Kyōbunkan, 1971, as vol. I of The Complete Works of Kanzō Uchimura.

disillusioned in his expectations, he ceased to shed those warm tears of joy which had flowed on first reaching the land of his dreams.

This chilling of the white heat of enthusiasm is nothing unusual. But Uchimura, interestingly, used Christian principles to fasten a moral critique on his experience of disillusionment. With his personal "American Dream" in tatters, he describes the cold American reality and his own painful feelings in somewhat exaggerated terms.

> The report that money was the almighty power in America was corroborated by many of our actual experiences. Immediately after our arrival at San Francisco, our faith in "Christian civilization" was severely tested by a disaster that befell one of our numbers. He was pickpocketed of a purse that contained a five-dollar-gold piece! "Pick-pocket-ing in Christendom as in Pagandom," we cautioned to each other.

Uchimura was also shocked that a black "church deacon" who kindly helped him with his luggage demanded a tip in return. Since the bell was loudly clanging the train's departure, those in the group could do nothing but give the man fifty cents each to get their bags back. The Japanese looked at each other in amazement and said, "Even charity is bartered here."

A year later, he boarded a pleasure ship in Massachusetts and there had his new silk umbrella stolen. Uchimura, struggling to get through school, was enraged.

> Here upon Christian waters, in a floating palace, under the spell of the music of Handel and Mendelssohn, things were as unsafe as in a den of robbers.

The urge to revile "Christian" America, by reflex caused him to praise the Orient of his birth. Moreover, while writing How I Became Christian, he was envisioning an audience of American readers who knew little of East Asia. Thus, Uchimura mingled fact and fancy, making some rather strange statements. "Even the Chinese civilization of forty centuries ago could boast of a state of society where nobody picked up things dropped on the street." Mixing wrath over his stolen umbrella with pride in his own country, he asserts:

> We in our heathen homes have but very little recourse to keys. Our houses, most of them, are open to everybody. Cats come in and out at their own sweet pleasures, and men go to siesta in

> their beds with zephyrs blowing over their faces . . . But things are quite otherwise in Christendom. Not only are safes and trunks locked, but doors and windows of all descriptions, chests, drawers, ice-boxes, sugar-vases, all . . . A bachelor coming home in the evening has first to thrust his hand into his pocket to draw out a cluster of some twenty or thirty keys to find out one which will open to him his lonely cell.

It might be interesting to take a closer look at Uchimura's preoccupation with the use of locks in America.

If one lives in a closely knit community where everyone knows one another, locks might not be necessary, but certainly locks and keys are necessary to anyone who is on the road. Also, in today's large cities where there is a possibility of unlocked cars being used for crimes, it might even be said that forgetting to lock up is an anti-social act.

But even while realizing that the use of lock and key is only natural, it was an odd feeling for me to see a lock on the telephone in the house where I boarded while in Europe. It was as though right from the start the landlady suspected I might make long-distance calls without permission. Even more, when visiting a Western missionary's home in Japan they see a lock on the refrigerator, most Japanese—not only men like Uchimura Kanzō—feel rather strange. In The Japanese and The Jews,[3] Isaiah Ben Dasan explains why Japanese are liable to misinterpret the use of locks and keys.

Ben Dasan notes that Christians operate from the assumption that man is basically sinful and easily subject to temptation. Thus, creating an environment where people can easily yield to temptation—say, a refrigerator one can easily steal from—is considered wrong. Uchimura loudly criticized Westerners' use of locks only to keep men honest. Ben Dasan notes that in America salesmen sell cash registers saying, "This is a machine that keeps people honest." In Japan this type of advertisement does not work. A Japanese shopkeeper would say, "I use a cash register so that there'll be no chance of suspecting a person unjustly and thus hurting his feelings."

When one notes the differences among cultural spheres, the differences in the ways of thinking become obvious, but this problem does not always have a direct bearing on moral superiority or inferiority. The anthropologist Ishida Eiichirō notes the differences between "Lock and Key Cultures and Fusuma

3. Isaiah Ben Dasan, The Japanese and the Jews (Yamamoto shoten, 1970); English translation, John Weatherhill & Co.

(sliding door) Culture."[4] He points out that most of Asia, including China, belongs to the lock-and-key cultural sphere, while Japan is unique in this regard. Locks were already evident in writings of China's Chou and Han periods, and the one who held the keys was the one who wielded the real power in the household. Nakane Chie elaborates on "Japan, the lockless culture" in Tekiō no jōken.[5] Professor Nakane discusses the experience of a Japanese girl who went to teach at a kindergarten in an Indian farming village:

> This girl noted that at the kindergarten boxes for books and other articles were always locked up, and thought it deplorable that even at such a young age things would disappear if not under lock and key. "We must teach children not to take things even when not locked up." She saw this as her mission. For that whole year she did everything she could to persuade the children that even without a lock things would not be stolen. At last, however, her efforts were fruitless and she disparingly returned to Japan.
>
> Ignorance of the cultural system of the land she was in resulted in a great loss of energy for her and the imposition of a foreign system of her pupils. In India, locking things up does not necessarily imply fear that someone will steal them, that others are wicked. A person puts on a lock when he wants to indicate, "It'll be inconvenient if someone borrows this without my knowledge. I'd like this left as it is." Even in a large household where only intimate family members and trusted servants may be living, the locking of closets and drawers containing personal belongings is the usual thing.

Though I agree with Professor Nakane's opinion, I would like to point out in passing that even among people of "lock-and-key" cultures the use of locks may be accompanied by a sense of wrong. For example, in the masterpiece of French juvenile literature, Sans Famille, the child Remi arrives in Paris and enters the Garofoli household. During Mr. Garofoli's absence, one of the children was looking after the house. A large pot was left hanging in the fireplace, and the soup in it was aboil, but there was a lock on the lid, so that the child would not take any of the soup. It is a scene which evokes much pity from the reader, because although Mr. Garofoli has not returned home yet,

4. Ishida Eiichiro, Ningen to bunka no tankyū (Man and the Pursuit of Culture), Bungei shunjū, 1970, pp. 106-9.
5. Nakane Chie, Tekiō no jōken (The Condition of Adaptation), Kōdansha, 1972, pp. 32-33.

the lock is a presentiment of his cold personality and of children crying from hunger. Thus, needless to say, it is not only a Japanese who can feel this way about locks.

But be that as it may, did Uchimura Kanzō really have good cause to assert that an American household

> is a miniature feudal castle modified to meet the prevailing cupidity of the age. Whether a civilization which requires cemented cellars and stone-cut vaults, watched over by bulldogs and battalions of policemen, could be called Christian is seriously doubted by honest heathens.

There are certainly people both among Americans and among Japanese who would seriously doubt whether Uchimura's criticism of Christian civilization is really a valid one. However, regardless of whether or not How I Became a Christian has objective relevance, when read as a glimpse into one man's psyche, it is a most interesting document. Taking a glance at Uchimura's subjective world, we might ask ourselves how to account for the drastic change in the image he had of America.

Less than one year after he arrived in America, he wrote to his father Uchimura Nobuyuki, "I have to say that no matter what our Japan is awful, awful, awful."[6] When he returned to Japan four years later, did he completely forget this sentiment and the other criticisms he wrote of Japan in comparison to America?

Since American society itself did not change so drastically at the time, what so greatly swayed Uchimura's judgement was not so much an objective image of American society as it really was, but rather his own subjectively projected image of America--and of Japan. Japan enters our consideration at this point because as his image of America declined his image of Japan and Asia rose accordingly. By going to the United States, he was forced to become conscious of his being a member of "the yellow race," a Japanese. The word "race" is used quite often in How I Became A Christian. At times he uses "race" seemingly interchangeably with words like "nation" and "people." Resentment, rooted in the heart of race-conscious Uchimura, was not much exacerbated by the black racial problem in America, but as a member of the yellow race he was enraged by the exclusion of Chinese from the flow of immigrants to America. Always of an easily inflamed nature, Uchimura gave vent to his wrath in the face of the problem:

6. Letter to Uchimura Nobuyuki, August 9, 1885.

> But strong and unchristian as their feeling is against the Indians and the Africans, the prejudice, the aversion, the repugnance, which they entertain against the children of Sina are something which we in heathendom have never seen the like. The land which sends over missionaries to China, to convert her sons and daughters to Christianity from the nonsense of Confucius and the superstitions of Buddha,—the very same land abhors even the shadow of a Chinaman cast upon its soil. There never was seen such an anomaly upon the face of this earth. Is Christian mission a child's play, a chivalry more puerile than that engaged the wit of Cervantes, that it should be sent to a people so much disliked by the people who sent it?

In Uchimura's criticism can be heard a cry of opposition to Western religious imperialism. Uchimura offers three reasons why Chinese were hated in America:

> 1. The Chinese carry all their savings to their home, and thus impoverish the land.

Standing in the position of the Americans at that time, one sees that the fact they and their forebearers came from Europe with the intention of living and dying on American soil made them fundamentally different from any Chinese laborers. It is easy to see then how salaries and savings could become an emotional issue.

> 2. The Chinese with their stubborn adherence to their national ways and customs, bring indecencies upon the Christian community.

Uchimura counters with another point of view:

> True, pigtails and flowing pantaloons are not very decent things to be seen in the streets of Boston or New York. But do you think corsets and compressed abdomens are fine things to see in the streets of Peking or Hankow?

Lastly, the third reason Uchimura refers to is the friction between immigrant and native labor.

> 3. The Chinese by their low wages do injury to the American laborer.

In a certain sense, today's "protection policy ethic" might be seen as related to this problem.

The history of Chinese exclusionism in America, from the California Gold Rush to the massacre of Chinese at Rock Spring, Wyoming, on September 2, 1885, is sketched succinctly in Wakatsuki Yasuo's Hainichi no rekishi.[7] The Governor of Wyoming reported to the federal government that at the Rock Spring Massacre, sixteen Chinese were beaten to death, up to sixty corpses recovered from the burnt buildings, and innumerable bodies unrecoverable. Since enraged mobs were still rampaging he requested the help of troops. After this incident, a number of suspects were arrested but all were released by a court for lack of evidence.

These events took place a year after Uchimura arrived in America in 1884. Two years before he arrived, the Chinese Exclusion Act went into effect for a term of ten years. Then in 1892, just before he wrote How I Became a Christian, this act was renewed. As a member of the "yellow race" Uchimura could not consider this problem as having no relation to himself. Burning with righteous indignation, he offers some proposals:

> Go to some more lordly occupations befitting your Teutonic or Celtic origin. Let them (the Chinese) wash all your cuffs and collars and shirts for you; and they will serve you with lamblike meekness, and for half the price your own Caucasian laundrymen charge you with. . . . "Strike" is yet unknown among the poor heathens, unless some of you teach them how to do it. A class of laborers so meek, so uncomplaining, so industrious, and so cheap, you cannot find anywhere else under the sun.

Uchimura was hoping for an America where not just those of Anglo-Saxon descent, but also Irish and Chinese could live and prosper together. And he believed that this hope would be consistent with his own view of Christianity.

But was this seemingly humanistic point of view really practicable? People of different cultural traditions trying to live as "one, big, happy family" form a rather difficult situation. Is not this, along with worries about "cheap labor," a factor in present-day Japan's tight controls on immigration despite a labor shortage?

7. Wakatsuki Yasuo, Hainichi no rekishi (The Anti-Japanese Movement in the U.S.), Chūō kōronsha, 1972.

America and Japan, Japan and China, China and America—in the sphere of international politics, since 1945 Japan has been bound in an "American-Japanese" relation. But earlier, during the 1930s and the Second World War, American sympathies were drawn toward China, as the popularity at the time of Pearl Buck's The Good Earth illustrates. The "American-Chinese" bond was quite strong. This sort of grouping is possible on a more personal level as well.

We have seen already Uchimura's longings for America, "the Holy Land." Because this bond had a religious basis, it was in some ways stronger and deeper than the ties of other Japanese students overseas. But because of the "culture shock" and his growing self-awareness as an Asian, a revision of his value judgments took place. He became eager to revive the ancient bonds between Japan and China and to push anti-Americanism into the foreground of his attitude toward his "second homeland."

In 1902, the entry of Chinese immigrants into America was completely forbidden, but after the Russo-Japanese War (1904-1905), the entry of Japanese immigrants too became in various ways a critical issue between Japan and America. Infuriated by laws forbidding land purchases by Japanese in California (1913) and limiting Japanese immigration (1924), Uchimura wrote a number of fiery newspaper articles at the time. If we select from his writings certain statements and combine them with a collection of the trends of those times, it might not be too difficult to construct an image of "Uchimura Kanzō, the Anti-Americanist." (I have even heard that an attempt was made a generation ago to gather from his writings a series of statements which would seem to support the aims of the Greater East Asian Co-Prosperity Sphere.)

Right after Congress passed the Immigation Act of 1924 containing the anti-Japanese provisions, he renewed his relationship with Tokutomi Sohō—later to become a chief ideologue of the "Greater East Asian War"—and sent a letter to the newspaper, Kokumin Shinbun, of which Tokutomi was editor.

> I completely agree with your opinions regarding the difficulties with America, Mr. Tokutomi. I am happy to be reading the Kokumin Shinbun again as I did thirty years ago. . . . There is no reason at all to fear America. . .[8]

8. See also Uchimura's letter to Tokutomi Roka, younger brother of Tokutomi Sohō, August 16, 1924.

But for all his ranting about America's attitude toward the Chinese, it is of great interest to note that he himself was insulted when mistaken for a Chinese. In How I Became A Christian, he writes:

> I am never ashamed of my racial relationship to that most ancient of nations,—that nation that gave Mencius and Confucius to the world, and invented the mariner's compass and printing machines centuries before the Europeans even dreamed of them.

But it nevertheless infuriated him when he himself was identified with the "coolies from Canton." He gives example after example of the slights he received—or thought he received. He recalls ironically the "polite language" of an Irish coachman in Chicago who called out something about "Chinamen" when picking up Uchimura and his group of fellow Japanese travelers. A well-dressed man sitting next to him in a coach asked to borrow his comb, and instead of thanking him after combing his "grizzly beard," he asked, "Well, John, where do you keep your laundry shop?" At another time, an intelligent looking gentleman asked him and his group when they cut their queues. Whey they told him that they had never had any queues he replied, "Why, I thought all Chinamen have queues." To Uchimura, each exchange seemed to be a sign of unbearable contempt and whenever he heard such comments he became terribly annoyed. Many Japanese of the time had this sort of pride and he notes the following anecdote with great relish:

> A group of young Japanese engineers went to examine the Brooklyn Bridge. When under the pier, the structure and tension of each of the suspending ropes were being discussed upon, a silk-hatted, spectacled, and decently dressed American gentleman approached them. "Well John," he intruded upon the Japanese scientists, "these things must look awful strange to you from China, ey!" One among the Japanese retorted the insulting question, and said, "So they must be to you from Ireland." The gentleman got angry and said, "No, indeed not. I am not an Irish." "And so we are not Chinese," was the gentle rejoinder. It was a good blow, and the silk-hatted sulked away.

This episode recalls a similar one involving Okakura Tenshin. Possibly because he had heard the question many times before, when once asked, "Are you a Chinese, Javanese or Japanese?", he promptly replied, "Are you a donkey, monkey or Yankee?" Though this type of ready repartee scores admirably, both in Okakura's case and in Uchimura's, did the one who asked the question really do so with such bad will? The very replies to these questions seem somewhat ill-natured. To demand that Westerners recognize the difference between Japanese and Chinese is rather unreasonable. In Japan today, all Westerners are usually taken for Americans, but this too is no cause for them to get angry, either.

The sight of him who had sided with the Chinese because of the Exclusion Act now suddenly disdaining to be associated with them creates a strange impression. That he felt displeasure at being mistaken for Chinese while in America is a fact which appears even in letters to his father:

> Everywhere I go I'm taken for a Chinaman, and it really annoys me. (December 21, 1884)
>
> Everywhere I am looked on as a Chinaman, and no matter where I go I'm jeered at. I can't tell you how painful it is. (August 9, 1885)

While this is apparently indicative of racial discrimnation, Ōta Yūzō notes in his recent study of Uchimura that this might not be entirely so.[9] We should recall, he explains, that Uchimura's feelings were due also to the humiliation he felt at being identified with manual laborers, while he was in reality a holder of an official position with the Japanese government.

But be that as it may, this sort of inconsistency between what he said and how he felt might be a characteristic peculiar to Uchimura. His indignation was the result of a strong tendency toward self-justification, but what kept it from becoming obnoxious was the echo of an almost comical rhetorical overstatement in the background. In the exaggerated manner of expression, a bit of Anglo-Saxon humor can be felt, due in part, perhaps, to the influence of the satiric tradition in English literature. There was something about him which enabled him to speak more frankly and freely when speaking in English to Americans than when speaking in Japanese. This might have been because his emotional life was to a large extent cultivated through the medium of the English language. Also, speaking in a high-flown tone of voice enabled him to parade his anger and hurt feelings and pout before his American friends. No doubt this was because he thought, "If they're friends, they're supposed to understand why I'm angry."

Many young Japanese who read this book might say in indignation, "American is a shameful place, a land of racial prejudice." But perhaps most

9. Ōta Yūzō, Uchimura Kanzō, p. 36.

human beings have a little of the Uchimura Kanzō within them. When it suited him, he supported the Chinese, but when his own pride became involved he too was willing to discriminate. The righteous indignation of a man with a strong sense of self-justification is somehow laughable, and most adults will see through his contentions. A man who cries, "We don't have racial prejudice like Americans," is himself guilty of prejudice--a prejudice called "anti-Americanism." Was not the psychological background for Uchimura's critique of America somewhat similar to that which provided the dynamics for Japanese anti-Americanism after the Second World War?

In the sixth and seventh chapters of How I Became a Christian, Uchimura Kanzō explained his yearning for America before he arrived there and the feeling of a need to return to things Japanese which was born during his stay in America.

> That I looked upon Christendom and English-speaking peoples with peculiar reverence was not an altogether inexcusable weakness on my part. It was the same weakness that made the Great Frederick of Prussia a slavish adorer of everything that was French. I learnt all that was noble, useful, and uplifting through the vehicle of the English language.

Uchimura had studied German language and literature while in Ameica, and knew something about the cultural history of Germany in the 18th century; he knew enough to try to excuse his past infatuation with western culture by making reference to Frederick's adoration of French culture. However, what is more important to us in connection with Uchimura's study of German culture is that he must have learned not only about the period of slavish imitation of French culture at the time of Frederick but also about the blossoming of German culture at the time of Goethe and Schiller, which was a direct result of discovery of the value of their own culture and subsequent cultural self-assertion of the German people. By knowing this precedent in German cultural history, Uchimura must have been helped to gain a greater confidence in his own culture. In this, I believe we catch a glimpse of the psychology behind Uchimura Kanzō's return to things Japanese.

Interestingly enough, Mori Ōgai referred to the same example during the time of his studies in Germany. A year younger than Uchimura, he traveled to the West in the same year he did, 1884, and emphasized his identity as a Japanese in his notes, Eindrucke, written during his stay in Germany:

> Preservation of nationality. Opposed to "substituting English for Japanese, Yomiuri Shinbun." German culture. Frederick the Great's disdain for the Geman language and worship of the French, a perversion. The flowering of the German spirit after Goethe and Schiller. "There is a beautiful literature in Japan. We must avoid replacing Japanese with another language."—Civilization stands on historical foundation. Even if you bring ready-made Western ideals to Japan, it is an impossibility to realize them there in the same way.

The beginning of the second decade of the Meiji period saw the casting away of some of the first decade's enthusiasm for Europeanization. In the seventh chapter of How I Became a Christian, Uchimura explains the loss of his fullhearted devotion to Western civilization and his rediscovery of Japan as follows:

> It was well said by a Chinese sage that "he who stays in a mountain knows not the mountain." . . . So with one's own country. As long as he lives in it, he really knows it not. That he may understand its true situation, it as part of the great whole, its goodness and badness, its strength and weakness, he must stand away from it.

The reference to the Chinese sage and proverb long familiar in Japan seems almost emblematic of his "back to the East" sentiments. Uchimura continues:

> "Send your darling son to travel," is a saying common among my countrymen. Nothing disenchants a man so much as traveling.
>
> My views about my native land were extremely one-sided while I stayed in it. While yet a heathen, my country was to me the centre of the universe, the envy of the world. . . . But how opposite when I was "converted"! I was told of "happy lands far, far away"; of America, with four-hundred colleges and universities; of England, the Puritan's home; of Germany, Luther's Fatherland; of Switzerland, Zwingli's pride; of Knox's Scotland and Adolphus' Sweden. Soon an idea caught my mind that my country was really "good-for-nothing." . . . Speaking of any of its moral or social defects, we were constantly told that it was not so in America or Europe. Whether it could ever be a Massachusetts or an England, I sincerely doubted.

What Uchimura says might seem a bit strange to a person unfamiliar with or unsympathetic to the deep cultural inferiority felt toward the west by many Japanese intellectuals of the time. The following reflections might appear rather commonplace, but they are indicative of Uchimura's feelings toward his overseas experience.

> Under no other circumstances are we driven more into ourselves than when we live in a strange land. Paradoxical though it may seem, we go into the world that we may learn more about ourselves. Self is revealed to us nowhere more clearly than where we come in contact with other peoples and other countries. Introspection begins when another world is presented to our view.

He noted how he who had once thought his country "good-for-nothing" once again took pride in it by being forced to behave as its representative.

> One is more than an individual when he steps out of his country. He carries in himself his nation and his race. His words and actions are judged not simply as his, but as his race's and his nation's as well. Thus in a sense, every sojourner in a strange land is a minister plenipotentiary of his country. He represents his land and his people. The world reads his nation through him. We know that nothing steadies a man so much as the sense of high responsibility.

Although his utterances show how violently his state of mind changed, this change was born not only of his recognition of Japan's value and based not only in self-confidence. It was also based on the sense of betrayal and disappointment derived from the dashing of his great expectations, a feeling that his love was cruelly unrequited. Just as a man rejected by a woman often starts acidly criticizing her whom he once loved, so Uchimura rages against industrialized American society.

> Peace is the last thing we can find in Christendom. Turmoils, complexities, insane asylums, penitentiaries, poor-houses!

Some American thinkers, too, were already making similar criticisms of American civilization. But we might note that at the time this book was written in 1893, there were no social welfare institutions in Japan at all, with the exception of Shibusawa Eiichi's poor-house. Full of pride as a Japanese, Uchimura sang of the beauties of agricultural Japan.

> O for the rest of the Morning Land, the quietude of the Lotus Pond! Not the steam-whistle that alarms us from our disturbed sleep, but the carol of the Bird of Paradise that wakens us from our delicious slumber; not the dust and jar of an elevated railroad, but a palanquin borne by a lowing cow; not marble-mansions built with the price of blood earned in the Wall Street battle-market, but thatched roofs with sweet contentment in Nature's bounties.

When they visited the old European continent, Americans like Mark Twain used to boast of the still-uncontaminated pure soul of "American innocence," in contrast to the decay and decadence of European civilization. William Dean Howells once wrote in a letter to one of his friends that "no one knows how much better than the whole world America is until he tries some other part of the world. Our people are manlier and purer than any in Europe."[10] Words similar to these were directed at America by Uchimura. We might call these sentiments about unspoiled Japan an expression of "Japanese innocence." However, can it really be said that the Japan he refers to is as "innocent" as might have been thought?

A reading of the thatched roofs and lotus ponds in this section of How I Became a Christian might suggest to us an "environmental hymn," flowing with anti-industrial romanticism, which anticipates the movement by eighty years. Even so, this is not the type of work one should accept at face value. Addressed to American readers, it was a work of self-assertion, denying the values of industrialized society. Because he presupposed American Christians as readers, Uchimura introduced the lotus pond, a symbol of Buddhism, to make American "Christian" society appear to suffer by comparison. Uchimura brags to his western readers, "Not the steam-whistle that alarms us from our disturbed sleep," but he knew very well that the call of the steam-whistle was indeed sounding throughout Meiji Japan too. And he also knew that this was a beautifully happy sound to the Japanese. When the people of the Meiji era, adults and children alike, sang the popular song about hearing the whistle as the train chugged out of Shinbashi Station, they were expressing not only a joy at setting out on a trip; but also joy at Japan's journey from an agricultural society to an industrialized one. In that Song of the Railroad[11] can be felt the almost childlike exuberance of the flowering of a new age of Japanese

10. Life in Letters of William Dean Howells (New York, Russel and Russel), vol. 1, p. 90.
11. The Song of the Railroad begins with the famous phrase "Kiteki issei Shimbashi o haya waga kisha wa hanaretari" (with a toot of the steam-whistle our train has already started from Shimbashi Station.)

civilization. Uchimura Kanzō directed one line of boasting toward westerners, but as an individual Japanese among his own countrymen he welcomed that call of the train whistle with all his heart.

In Chijin-ron, a treatise on geography written in Japanese shortly after How I Became a Christian, he celebrated the fact that in Japan, too, rails had been laid; and expressed pride in being Japanese—drawing China, it should be noted, into an unfavorable comparison. He writes in the ninth chapter of Chijin-ron:

> America sought our acquaintance, we welcomed it and shook its hand. Its culture quickly seeped into us. Japan, already having studied China and India to the fullest, with her innate powers of assimilation began to inhale the West. . . . When our neighbor to the West still had not one yard of railroad, a culture of miles and miles of steel road stretching to the remotest of places had already been imported here. In thirty years, Japan has become un-Oriental.[12]

At the time of the Sino-Japanese War in 1894, the railroad already reached from Shinbashi in Tokyo to Hiroshima. For that reason the General Headquarters of the Imperial Army was able to move to Hiroshima. No doubt the state of mind which caused Uchimura to celebrate, in contrast to China, Japan's turning away from Asia and toward the West was related to the nationalistic exaltation prevalent around the time of the Sino-Japanese war.

At any rate, we have seen a love-hate relationship at work in Uchimura's way of looking at things. Also, we have seen him affirming his unity with the yellow peoples at one time, and at other times denying this identity by affirming his own nationality according to the needs presented by each situation. When we consider how violent Uchimura's emotional states were we can easily see why such fierce anti-American feelings arose at the time the anti-Japanese immigration laws were passed. In articles he wrote for such influential newspapers as the Kokumin Shinbun and the Yomiuri Shinbun, we read such statements as:

> What America has is money. If you exclude money, America has almost nothing. It has neither philosophy nor art worth the name. The noble gentlemen who once were have now for the

12. Uchimura Kanzō zenshū (The Complete Works of Uchimura Kanzō), Iwanami shoten, 1932-33, I, p. 642.

> most part disappeared without a trace. It is no exaggeration to say that as a civilization, America minus money equals zero.[13]

Statements like this remind one of an Imperial Army officer addressing the troops on the eve of the Greater East Asian War in 1941.

Unlike other students who went to America in search of merely practical knowledge, Uchimura Kanzō looked at America within the framework of Christianity as a standard for value judgment. When he attempted to measure American society with this idealistic, ethical standard, he found various facts far removed from this standard. From this shock came his anti-American rhetoric. But despite his disappintment in America, he could not completely turn his back on it and break off all ties. While he could reject American industrial culture—at least on the surface—he could not cast Christianity away and return to his former self. On this point, Uchimura was different from "A Conservative" whom Lafcadio Hearn describes in Kokoro. Toward the end of the sixth chapter of How I Became A Christian, confronted with cold reality and fondly reminiscing about his departed grandmother, Uchimura exclaims:

> O heaven, I am undone! I was deceived! I gave up what was really Peace for that which is no Peace! To go back to my old faith I am now too ovegrown; to acquiesce in my new faith is impossible. O for blessed Ignorance that might have kept me from the knowledge of faith other than that which satisfied my good grandma! It made her industrious, patient, true; and not a compunction clouded her face as she drew her last breath. Hers was peace and mine is doubt; and woe is me that I called her an idolater, and pitied her superstition, and prayed for her soul, when I myself had launched upon an unfathomable abyss, tossed with fear and sin and doubt. One thing I shall never do in the future: I shall never defend Christianity upon its being the religion of Europe and America.

While revolt against Christian society in the West was expressed in terms of yearning for the old Japanese faith, it did not amount to a farewell to Christianity itself. The Christian faith had penetrated Uchimura too deeply for that. Kamei Shunsuke notes that this excerpt praising the "Blessed Ignorance" of Uchimura's grandmother resembles a verse in the fifteenth

13. Uchimura Kanzō chosakushū (Selected Works of Uchimura Kanzō), Iwanami shoten, 1953-55, IV, p. 372.

chapter of Jeremiah, a verse also quoted in Gaikokugo no kenkyū.[14] Let us compare the two excerpts:

> O heaven, I am undone! I was deceived. . . and woe is me that I called her an idolater, and pitied her superstition, and prayed for her soul, when I myself had launched upon an unfathomable abyss, tossed with fear and sin and doubt. (Uchimura)

> Woe is me, my mother, that thou hast borne me a man of strife and man of contention to the whole earth! I have neither lent on usury; nor men have lent to me on usury; yet every one of them doth curse me. (Jeremiah 15:10)

There appears to be a resemblance between the two passages in tone and rhythm. Regarding the influence of the Biblical style on Uchimura's English writings, Mr. Kamei suggests that "we should not look on this resemblance as a direct imitation. What is more important is the Bible's overall influence, which when it surfaces produces this type of similarity." It can easily be seen how with such a deep feeling for the scriptures Uchimura was unable to return to his old beliefs. He did indeed return to "things Japanese," but he could not accept his old Japan in its entirety. He remained strong in his resolve "never to defend Christianity upon its being the religion of Europe and America." This resolve was connected with his dislike of western missionaries and concealed in the ethical and psychological necessity he felt for starting the "Non-church Christianity" movement.

Christianity is a world religion. Or rather, as Uchimura follows his own convenient geography in essays like "Nihon to kirisutokyō," Christianity "started in Asia, . . . is most suited to Asia." "There is no mistake greater than calling Christianity a Western religion," "The West did not make Christianity," but rather "Christianity made the West." "Christianity in Japan has already born fruit different from that of the West." "The Christianity which has appeared through the Japanese" is what Uchimura called "Nihon-teki kirisutokyō"—a real Japanese Christianity.

In this way, Uchimura emphasized "Asia," a term originally used only as another word for "non-Western," but in reality having neither the religious nor cultural uniformity he seemed to suppose. But it was to Japan, the land of his birth and place where he could labor tirelessly, that his love belonged. For

14. Kamei Shunsuke, "Uchimura Kanzō to eigo" (Uchimura Kanzō and English) in Kokugo tsūshin (Chikuma shobō), no. 143.

Uchimura all was "for Japan," all was "for Jesus." When he composed the inscription for his tombstone in both English and Japanese, the first line read, "I love two J's and no third; one is Jesus, and the other is Japan."

But does this mean that he really had banished America completely from his heart? If so, one might ask with a slightly ironic smile, "Then why did Uchimura Kanzō have his grave inscription written not only in Japanese, but in English too? Whom did he want to read it?"

# UCHIMURA KANZŌ: THE CARLYLE OF JAPAN

Ōta Yūzō

Interest in Uchimura Kanzō in postwar Japan continues to grow unabated. The Japanese fascination with Uchimura is stimulated in part by the strong emotions that he provoked among his contemporaries as well as among scholars today. A recent biographer has written: "Some described him as a man of contradictions, and others as a great X (enigma)."[1] Such divergent views and evaluations have deepened the confusion that surrounds Uchimura and make it more difficult to form a satisfactory image of him. In retrospect, his contemporaries seem to have had a more sharply focused view of him. They had no difficulty in identifying him as the "Carlyle of Japan." While such characterizations may sound glib and are often misleading, this one has much to recommend it. Thomas Carlyle (1795-1881) was a renowned author whose writings had a special appeal to many former Japanese samurai, especially those who were distant from the seat of power and hostile to the Meiji government. Carlyle enjoyed a loyal following in Japan just as Uchimura emerged as a popular writer and journalist towards the end of the nineteenth century. This identification of him with Carlyle, which Uchimura himself came to accept, seems to me both apt and suggestive, for it points to several important traits of Uchimura as a man and as a writer which might help to reduce some of the mystery surrounding this enigmatic thinker of modern Japan. This essay is an attempt to demonstrate the nature and origins of some of these traits.

1. Masaike Jin, Uchimura Kanzō den (San'ichi shobō, 193), p. 2. Several new studies of Uchimura have recently appeared: Ohara Shin, Hyōden Uchimura Kanzō (Kanzō Uchimura: His Life and Thought) Chūō Kōronsha, 1976; Kamei Shunsuke, Uchimura Kanzō: Meiji seishin no dōhyō (Uchimura Kanzō: A signpost of the Meiji Spirit), Chūō Kōronsha, 1977; Azegami Michio, Ningen Uchimura Kanzō no tankyū: Sei to zoku to kyōki no aida de (Investigation of Uchimura Kanzō the Man: Between the Sacred, the Secular and the Insanity), Sanpō, 1977; and my own Uchimura Kanzō: Sono sekaishugi to Nihonshugi o megutte (World and Nation in Modern Japanese Christianity: The Case of Uchimura Kanzō) Kenkyūsha, 1977.

Uchimura was a person who could not find his mission in life for a long time. The decisive event in this respect was his move to Kyoto, Japan's ancient capital, in July 1893. There he started his career as a writer. By the end of his Kyoto period, which lasted for three years, he had established himself as a writer, and until the end of his life he remained a writer, although the subject matter of his writing changed over the years.

The decision to try to live as a writer was not an easy one for him. "Writing was what I had hated more than anything else," he later recalled.[2] Only when every other path seemed to be closed after his unsuccessful attempt to settle down in careers as a bureaucrat and as a teacher did he turn to writing. In a letter to D. C. Bell, his American friend, dated March 29, 1893, Uchimura disclosed for the first time his intention to move to Kyoto to start a writing career: "My friends advise me to go to letter (sic) where I can be with myself alone, and can teach the whole nation. They say I am a little Carlyle and am too erratic to go on with others."[3]

The reference to Carlyle indicates that when Uchimura decided to give up teaching and try his hand at writing, he was perhaps consciously following in the footsteps of that famous writer. Later Uchimura found in John Nichol's Thomas Carlyle the following sentences: "In 1818 Carlyle, always intolerant of work imposed, came to the conclusion that 'it was better to perish than to continue schoolmastering,' and left Kirkcaldy, with £90 saved, for Edinburgh, where he lived over three years, . . . trying to enter his real mission through the gate of literature." Uchimura underlined "it was better to perish than to continue schoolmastering," and wrote "yea!" in the margin.[4] He must have been struck with the strong similarity between himself and Carlyle.

2. Uchimura Kanzō zenshū (The complete Works of Uchimura Kanzō), Iwanami Shoten, 1932-33, XI, p. 218. Cited hereafter as Zenshū.
3. Zenshū, XX, p. 242. Uchimura's letters to D. C. Bell, all written in English, at times contain grammatical mistakes.
4. John Nichol, Thomas Carlyle (Harper Broters, N.Y., 1892), p. 24. Most of Uchimura's personal library was donated to Hokkaido University Library after his death, and is preserved there as the Uchimura Bunko. With the single exception of Correspondence of Thomas Carlyle and Ralph Waldo Emerson 1834-1872, ed. Charles Eliot Norton, all the books by and about Carlyle in this article refer to ones which were Uchimura's personal copies. They often contain useful comments, underlines and dates by Uchimura. For example, from "Kanzō Uchimura, Kyoto, Sept. 1895." and "Sept. 14, 1895" written at the beginning and the end of his copy of John Nichol's Thomas Carlyle respectively, we learn that Uchimura bought a copy of John Nichol's Thomas Carlyle in Kyoto in September 1895 and finished reading it on the fourteenth of the same month.

If Uchimura entered a writing career in conscious imitation of Carlyle, it is hardly surprising that he was seen as the Carlyle of Japan as soon as his writing became widely known in the last decade of the nineteenth century. "'The Carlyle of Japan,' 'A little Carlyle,' 'A second Carlyle,' —these are titles which the Kobe Herald and numerous magazines for young men have given me," Uchimura wrote in 1899.[5] At the time Uchimura was perhaps too ambitious to receive such epithets gladly; he wanted to be a great writer in his own right and not just an epigone or an imitator, although in reality he was strongly influenced by Carlyle as we shall see below. "Those he wrote who regard me as a disciple of Carlyle simply because I criticized present-day Japanese society are mistaken. I didn't do this in imitation of or at the instigation of Carlyle. I attacked hypocrisies and lies in Japanese society simply because I was an ordinary Japanese faithful to the teachings of our ancestors."[6] In his later years, however, Uchimura's attitude towards being regarded as the Carlyle of Japan became quite different.

In 1920 a friend visited Carlyle's birthplace in Scotland and sent a postcard to Uchimura from there, saying "Visiting these places I could not help thinking about you. Carlyle, I hear, was person who wore a hat with a black rim and who walked somewhat slanting forward. I thought that was like you. His face I thought was also like yours." Reading these words Uchimura "felt honored and happy."[7] Also, J. W. Robertson Scott described Uchimura as "a Carlyle" since "his fibre and resolution, downright way of writing and speaking, hortatory gift, humour, plainness of life and dislike of officials, no less than his cast of countenance, his soft hat and long gaberdine-like coat have suggested" such a resembance. Uchimura was very flattered and wrote in his diary (22 May 1922), "I am very happy. I gratefully accept this nickname (the Carlyle of Japan)."[8] His acceptance of it in his later years perhaps attests to his greater knowledge of himself.

His close co-worker, Azegami Kenzō, wrote after Uchimura's death: "Although Uchimura read widely, what made a dominant influence on Uchimura's English language writings both in content and form were the Old Testament (in English translation) and Carlyle's writings."[9] It is my opinion

5. Zenshū, II, p. 639.
6. Ibid., II, p. 639-40.
7. Ibid., XVII, p. 361.
8. J.W. Robertson Scott, The Foundations of Japan (John Murray, London, 1922), 91-92; Zenshū, XVII, p. 586.
9. Azegami Kenzō, "Uchimura Sensei no eibun," Uchimura Kanzō zenshū geppō, No. 14 (Iwanami Shoten, May 1933), p. 1.

that the influence of both extended to Uchimura's Japanese language writings as well. In the following pages I will demonstrate the extent of Carlyle's influence on Uchimura, discuss the nature of his influence, and evaluate Uchimura through his relationship with Carlyle.

Uchimura's former classmate at Sapporo Agricultural Collge, Nitobe Inazō (1862-1933), who later became Under-Secretary of the League of Nations and one of the foremost interpreters of Japan to the West, shared Uchimura's enormous enthusiasm for Carlyle. He claimed to have read Carlyle's Sartor Resartus thirty-four times.[10] Because of his friendship with Nitobe, Uchimura had been familiar with the name of Carlyle since Nitobe discovered him in 1880. Examination of Uchimura's personal copies of Carlyle's works, of references to Carlyle in his letters, in the few works Uchimura had written, and in Uchimura's later reminiscences, indicates that almost certainly before his move to Kyoto he had read Sartor Resartus, Heroes and Hero-Worship and Oliver Cromwell's Letter and Speeches. These works had already exerted important influence on Uchimra. Cromwell's Letters and Speeches was significant in connection with the lese majesty incident which Uchimura provoked on January 9, 1891. This famous incident occurred because Uchimura, who was then a teacher of the First Higher Middle School, entertained some scruples of conscience against bowing before the Imperial signature attached to the school's copy of the Imperial Rescript on Education. As a Christian Uchimura could not perform unthinkingly an act which resembled religious worship. Unlike his colleagues and students, he hesitated when his turn came and finally bowed only slightly, thus causing a tremendous furor. It is interesting to note in the present connection that Uchimura himself associated his "refusal" to bow with his reading of Carlyle's Oliver Cromwell's Letters and Speeches:

> As for the influence Carlyle's Oliver Cromwell's Letter and Speeches exerted on me, I cannot find adequate words to describe it. I bought a five volume edition published in Britain in Azabu Iikura, Tokyo. It was 1890, and I had just been hired by the First Higher Middle School as a part-time teacher (in September 1890). Once I started reading it, I was completely absorbed in it. Through this book the value of freedom and independence was brought home to me. When I reached about the middle of the book, I was told by Dr. X, the acting principal of the school, to bow deeply, as if in religious worhip, before the copy of the Imperial Rescript on Education which had been issued shortly

10. Nitobe Inazō zenshū, XI (Kyōbunkan, 1969), p. 418.

> before. However, at that time I was too much possessed by Carlyle and Cromwell to obey this order with the approval of my conscience.[11]

Uchimura called Oliver Cromwell's Letters and Speeches, "my second Bible," and confessed that "If I hadn't read this book, my life would have been entirely different."[12] The date "Nov. 11, 1890" written by Uchimura at the end of Vol. 11 of Oliver Cromwell's Letters and Speeches in the Uchimura Collection, suggests that his account is authentic. Sartor Resartus and Heroes and Hero-Worship were probably almost as important to Uchimura before his move to Kyoto. In these two books Carlyle exalted the mission of the writer. Deeds, he wrote, "greater than all recorded miracles have been performed by Pens. Men of Letters are a perpetual Priesthood, from age to age, teaching all men that a God is still present in their life."[13] As Uchimura read these words, underlining and making notes in the margins, his determination became firmer to pursue a writing career as the way to realize his mission in life. Perhaps without them Uchimura might never have gathered enough courage to embark on a literary career.

Despite Carlyle's considerable influence on him before he moved to Kyoto, Uchimura did not feel the full impact of Carlyle's writings on his life until his intensive study in Kyoto. During these years Uchimura saw Carlyle as (a) a model writer who revealed his secrets of writing and who was, as Uchimura explicitly acknowledged, "my master of the trade in which I am now only an apprentice" and (b) an example of an honest man trying to live true to himself.[14]

Uchimura had scant regard for the world of belles lettres. He allegedly read only one novel in his life. As for The Tale of Genji, almost unanimously regarded as the greatest work of classical Japanese literature, Uchimura thought that it had helped to make the Japanese effiminate and maintained that "such works should be rooted out from among us."[15] There was only one type of literary work that Uchimura could produce: the more or less naked confessions of the feelings and thoughts which his immediate experiences evoked. Beginning with Kirisuto shinto no nagusame (Consolations of a

11. Zenshū, XIX, pp. 130-131.
12. Ibid., XIX, p. 925.
13. Sartor Resartus (Chapman and Hall; London, 1893), p. 137; Heroes and Hero-Worship, p. 143.
14. Zenshū, XX, p. 319.
15. Ibid., XIX, p. 128; I, p. 347.

Christian) and Kyūanroku (Search after Peace) both dating from his pre-Kyoto years, almost all of Uchimura's early works were confessions of one kind or another.

At the beginning of his professional writing career Uchimura was still unsure of the value of his own writings. By reading Carlyle's works, however, he gained a surer sense that what he wrote was not without value. This we learn from a careful examination of marginal comments and underlinings left in his personal copies of Carlyle's works as well as from his published statements. For example, the following sentence from Heroes and Hero-Worship is underlined: "If a book come from the heart, it will contrive to reach other hearts; all art and authorcraft are of small amount to that." Also right at the beginning of his stay in Kyoto, Uchimura read Carlyle's Past and Present. His personal copy bears the words "Kanzō Uchimura, Suma (where Uchimura attended a summer school), 1893 Summer." On p. 43 he wrote: "Veracity, true simplicity of heart, how valuable are these always! He that speaks what is really in him will find men to listen, though under never such impediments." Uchimura used these words as a kind of motto in How I Became a Christian, which he was then writing. Needless to say, How I Became a Christian, with the subtitle of "Out of my Diary," is a strongly autobiographical work. "I have written so much about my personal experiences this year," he wrote to D. C. Bell toward the end of 1893, "that I have now no courage left to expose more of myself, at least for some time."[16] After creation of his personal magazine Seisho no kenkyū (The Biblical Study) in September 1900, Uchimura gradually confined himself to writing commentaries on the Bible. He thus wrote his works of enduring value to general readers before 1900, and he might not have written them at all without Carlyle's implied encouragement to write personal confessions.

During his Kyoto period Uchimura, "as ever an industrious student of Carlyle," as he confessed to D. C. Bell in 1896, read a great many works of Thomas Carlyle. Since Uchimura had the habit of writing the date of purchase of a book inside the front cover, and often, the date of finishing a book or a chapter, it is possible to trace fairly accurately his reading of Carlyle during these years. For example, all seven volumes of Carlyle's Critical and Miscellaneous Essays bear the words "Kanzō Uchimura. Kyoto, July 27, 1895," the date of purchase. To cite another example, at the end of "Boswell's Life of Johnson" in volume four of the Essays, we find the words "Kyoto, Aug. 9, 1895," the date on which Uchimura finished reading it. An examination of

16. Ibid., XX, p. 260.

Uchimura's personal copies of Carlyle's works reveals how deeply influenced he was by Carlyle's writings. At the beginning of "Boswell's Life of Johnson," for example, Uchimura wrote in English: "Read with tears and high sensibilities. O my soul, this!"

Altogether Carlyle was an indispensable companion while Uchimura was struggling to establish himself as a writer in Kyoto. As he wrote to friends, "With my Greek Testament, a set of Carlyle, and a little income supplied by a bookseller in this city sufficient to procure us rice and sweet potatoes, and meat thrice a week, I am a happy contented man." And, on another occasion, "My work-shop is a paradise as ever, with occasional calls from Zuku (the nickname of Uchimura's old friend who was then living in Kyoto) and few choice souls that are still left in this flunkey nation. Bible, Carlyle, and few theologians and scientists! Enough that so much are still left unto me."[17] As these quotations indicate, toward the end of his days in Kyoto, Uchimura's letters began to sound an optimistic note as he developed confidence in himself as a writer; they reveal the very important position Carlyle occupied in Uchimura's life.

The constant reading of Carlyle's works in Kyoto and for a few years thereafter left a clear mark on Uchimura's own writings of that time. Sentences like "Read with tears and high sensibilities. O my soul, this!" already smack strongly of Carlyle. Uchimura's Japan and the Japanese, the second English language book which he wrote in Kyoto, abounds in such Carlylean sentences as " 'Be a saint,' —What an amibition this!" and "A modest, unseen business, this of school-teaching."[18] An examination of Carlyle's essay on "Biography" in the fourth volume of Critical and Miscellaneous Essays in the light of Uchimura's marginal comments, underlinings, and a date in his personal copy clearly reveals that this essay was an important source of inspiration for Uchimura's "Ikani shite dai-bungaku o en ka" (How to Make Great Literature), published in the October 12, 1895, issue of Kokumin no tomo. On the first page of "Biography" Uchimura wrote in big letters, "The Gospel of Literary Men." In "How to Make Great Literature," Uchimura quoted from "Biography" a passage which advised: "Sweep away utterly all frothiness and falsehood from your heart; struggle unweariedly to acquire, what is possible for every god-created Man, a free, open, humble soul: speak not at all, in any wise, till you have somewhat to speak; care not for the reward of your speaking" (p. 64). He wrote in the margin next to the

17. Ibid., XX, pp. 307, 313.
18. Ibid., XV, pp. 273, 276.

original paagraph in his personal copy of Carlyle's essay, "O my Soul! Great these! (sic)" It is also very easy to see that Uchimura's "Jisei no kansatsu" (The Signs of the Times), published in the August 15, 1896, issue of Kokumin no tomo, an explosive success which won wide recognition for the author, was written under the inspiration of Carlyle's own "The Signs of the Times." Uchimura himself said in a letter to D. C. Bell dated March 8, 1896: "The inspiration came as usual from the Holy Writ and Thomas Carlyle."[19] These are a few examples. A detailed examination of Carlyle's influence on Uchimura on the basis of careful comparison of their individual works might be well worth attempting.

Looking back on his three years in Kyoto, Uchimura wrote to D. C. Bell in October 1896, "But ah! the hunger and struggle of the last three years. I tell you, it was terrible." Uchimura in his Kyoto period saw himself like Carlyle early in his career, struggling to earn an honest living by writing. But at the same time he was immensely attracted by Carlyle the man when he came to know more about his life. In a letter to D. C. Bell dated July 24, 1895, Uchimura wrote, "I read Dante and much of Thomas Carlyle. . . The latter I imagine to be the sincerest man of this generation. . . I was recently reading Carlyle-Emerson Correspondence, and I felt as if I was reading my own diary."[20]

The Carlyle-Emerson Correspondence referred to here must be Correpondence of Thomas Carlyle and Ralph Waldo Emerson 1834-1872, edited by Charles Eliot Norton and first published in Boston in 1883. The following quotations from this book were used in Uchimura's letter just cited: "Now forty (thirty-five in my case) years of age; and extremely dyspeptical; a hopeless-looking man.—Where the money I have lived on has come from while I sat here scribbling gratis, amazes me to think; yet surely it has come (for I am still here,) and heaven only to thank for it,—which is a great fact." The expression, "Thirty-five in my case," was of course inserted by Uchimura by way of a note. The first quotation ("Now. . . a hopeless-looking man.") is taken from Carlyle's letter dated April 29, 1836, and the second from a letter of November 5, 1836, when Carlyle was just beginning to establish himself.

In 1896 Uchimura bought James Anthony Froude's massive four-volume biography of Carlyle.[21] To D. C. Bell Uchimura wrote about this book:

19. Ibid., XX, p. 315.
20. Ibid., XX, pp. 335, 296-97.
21. Thomas Carlyle: A History of the First Forty Years of His Life, 1795-

> I am now reading Froude's "Life of Carlyle." It is a book (4 vols.) which to a struggling writer is a veritable evangel. I wish you would some day in your leisure make it your own reading. You will find therein a genuine son of Puritanic fath, a thorough Scotch, who will not sell his soul for anything this world offered for his talent. If Carlyle was not an Orthodox Christian, he was the greatest preacher of Righteousness the century has had,--the nearest approach to Jeremiah or Ezekiel that this materialistic century can ever make.[22]

To his friend Nitobe Inazō, Uchimura wrote on the same date:

> Am now reading Froude's "Thomas Carlyle," 4 vol. 1000 pages of solid printing. One of the most readable books I ever have read. Therein is the real Carlyle, it seems so to me,--honest, struggling "tearful Tom." He is the best companion I have now. Can an honest man, with simple trust in God and himself, go through this selfish, clothes-worshipping, money-worshipping world, without trusting in anybody else. Carlyle with his struggling life of four-score-years answers Yea. Why cannot I then, I say to myself and get courage.[23]

These quotations reveal that the main bond that Uchimura felt with Carlyle the man was that they were both strong individuals struggling almost single-handedly in a corrupt and hostile world.

In January 1898 Uchimura gave a talk with the title, "Kārairu o manabu no ri to gai" (Advantages and Disadvantages of Studying Carlyle). He had by this time become a very prestigious journalist in Tokyo and was almost universally regarded as the "Carlyle of Japan." In this talk he discussed not only the good influence but also the bad influence Carlyle could exert upon his readers. The benefits included things like "belief in the importance of sincerity," "high esteem for work," and "love of the poor." He especially stressed that one could learn the value of sincerity from Carlyle.[24]

1835, 2 Vols., (Harper & Brothers, N.Y., n.d.), hereafter cited as First Forty Years; and Thomas Carlyle: A History of His Life in London, 1834-1881, 2 Vols., (Harper & Brothers, N.Y., 1885), hereafter Life in London.
22. Zenshū, XX, pp. 318-19.
23. Ibid., XX, p. 321.
24. Ibid., XIX, pp. 10-13.

As for the disadvantages, Uchimura stressed that Carlyle tended to make his readers dissatisfied with everything:

> The harm one receives as soon as one starts studying Carlyle is that one gets dissatisfied. Everything comes to appear wrong. Nothing satisfies one. Nothing comes up to one's ideal. The behaviour of the neighbors one observes daily is disgusting. What one observes in politics makes one indignant. If one reads literary works which come out one after another, one only feels like attacking them all mercilessly. If one goes to church, one does not feel any peace. One cannot suppress discontent towards the pastor and church members. One's temper and heart become rough. One can no longer observe the bright side of things. Focusing one's eyes only on the dark side of things, one comes to feel indignation at everything and attack everything.[25]

Despite the dangers Uchimura himself remained an avid reader of Carlyle. Was he free from the fuheibyō (discontent disease) that he believed reading Carlyle tended to cause? In fact, while warning others not to catch this "disease" from Carlyle, Uchimura was busily denouncing Japan as "corrupted, corrupted, how corrupted is the present-day Japanese society! The aristocracy is corrupted. The common people are corrupted. Officials are corrupted. Members of the House of Representatives are corrupted, Buddhist monks are corrupted, Christian pastors are corrupted, students are corrupted."[26] His choice of pen names or pseudonyms around this time is quite characteristic of his state of mind. He used, for example, "Shō fungaisei" (Little indignant fellow), "Fuheisei" (Discontented fellow), "Rippukusei" (Angry Fellow), and "Kanshakusei" (A fellow who loses his temper). In the January 1901 issue of Chūō Kōron, a writer called Kōdō characterized Uchimura as follows:

> In this world there are people who start weeping when drunk and people who start laughing when drunk. Mr. Uchimura is close to the first group of people. Whatever he sees and whatever he hears breed in him discontent and dissatisfaction, and he spends the whole day giving vent to his anger and discontent. From such a person we can expect only attacks, destructive criticisms—in short, what, at best, helps to destroy what should be destroyed. For the work of construction he is utterly unsuited.

25. Ibid., XIX, pp. 14-15.
26. Ibid., II, p. 940.

Thus, in the eyes of some, Uchimura looked very much like an example of a person with the very "discontent disease" against which he had warned others. This, however, was probably one secret of his literary success around this time.

Uchimura's emergence as a writer of national importance came shortly after Japan's victory over China in the Sino-Japanese War, which was concluded by the Treaty of Shimonoseki in April 1895. The victory was to many Japanese a symbolic event signifying at least a partial fulfillment of the major goal Japan had been striving for since the Meiji Restoration--the goal of making Japan rich and strong. The Japanese gained greatly in self-confidence. However, the euphoric mood in which even a person like Fukuzawa Yukichi indluged himself ("How happy I am; I have no words to express it! Only because I have lived long, I have met this wonderful joy. Why, then, couldn't all my friends live to meet it? I am often brought to tears of pity for those who died too soon.") could easily degenerate into self-complacency.[27] However, there were people who were in no mood to be complacent, people who chafed under the growing ridigity and conservatism of the Meiji government under a succession of cabinets led by elder statesmen from former Chōshū and Satsuma han. To them Uchimura's bold attack on "everybody" and "everything" might well have been a source of great vicarious pleasure. "Everybody now talks about the greatness of Japan. I alone want to discuss her smallness," he wrote in "Signs of the Times."[28] This militant tone was to be characteristic of many of Uchimura's writings during the years after Japan's victory over China.

If the "discontent disease" was not entirely an unmixed curse, the sincerity which Uchimura so much admired in Carlyle and which he wanted himself and others to emulate was very likely not entirely an unmixed blessing, either. In fact, although Uchimura did not suspect this, the advantages and disadvantages of studying Carlyle were closely related and almost inseparable. In Heroes and Hero-Worship (p. 67) Carlyle, discussing Mahomet, wrote: "No Dilettantism in this Mahomet; it is a business of Reprobation and Salvation with him, of Time and Eternity: He is in deadly earnest about it! Dilettantism, hypothesis, speculation, a kind of amateur-search for Truth, toying and coqueting with Truth: this is the sorest sin." In his personal copy

27. The Autobiography of Yukichi Fukuzawa, tran. Eiichi Kiyooka (Shocken Books, New York, 1972), p. 355.
28. Zenshū, II, p. 314.

Uchimura underlined the part beginning with the second 'Dilettantism." In Heroes and Hero-Worship there are numerous other places where Carlyle preaches the importance of sincerity and earnestness. However, according to Uchimura, Heroes and Hero-Worship was, of all the works of Carlyle, the one "which would exert the greatest amount of bad influences upon its readers."[29] Apparently Uchimura did not notice the incongruent fact that the work which preaches sincerity perhaps more than any other work of Carlyle was at the same time the one which provoked a pervasive feeling of discontent in its readers.

A contemporary of Carlyle said of him, "He is a lover of earnestness more than a lover of truth."[30] This appears to be a very apt evaluation. What one sincerely believes in could be mistaken. Subjective earnestness is no guarantee that something is objectively true. Arishima Takeo, one of the major writers of modern Japan, recorded in his diary after paying a visit to Uchimura: "I cannot help holding my peace before him whenever I see him. His will makes his mistaken ideas pass for truth."[31] Is it not possible that Uchimura received a rather baleful influence from Carlyle's excessive emphasis on sincerity? A cult of sincerity seems to lead to excessive exaltation of self.

At the beginning of this essay we saw that Uchimura's friends thought that he was a little Carlyle and was too erratic to get along with others. In fact, Uchimura was notorious for his tendency to quarrel with those around him unless they accepted him as the indisputable center of the group. "The story of Mr. Uchimura's life until today is a story of quarrelling with others. Everywhere he quarrelled with others. Quarrelling can be justified at times, but his perpetual quarrelling makes us wonder if his character does not leave much to be desired," wrote a contemporary critic.[32] Carlyle had a similar egotistic trait even to a greater degree. Commenting on his tendency to dominate others around him, Froude wrote: "It is perfectly true that Carlyle would have been an unbearable inmate of any house, except his father's, where his will was not absolute."[33] Like Uchimura, Carlyle could not tolerate those who disagreed with him and "when contradicted was contemptuous and overbearing."[34] Uchimura once said, comparing Carlyle and Nietzche: "Nietzche

29. Ibid., XIX, p. 9.
30. John Nichol, Thomas Carlyle, p. 30.
31. Arishima Takeo Zenshū (Shinchōsha, 1929), p. 214.
32. Kōdō, "Kyōkai jimbutsu gettan Uchimura Kanzō shi," Chūō Kōron, Jan. 1901, p. 29.
33. First Forty Years, I, p. 202.
34. Life in London, I, p. 2.

resembled Carlyle, but he and Carlyle were different in one important point; Carlyle acknowledged his frailty and depended on One who was greater than himself. Nietzche knew his own frailty, but he did not acknowledge it and wanted to stand up in this infinite universe by himself, although he was a frail mortal."[35] However, even if Carlyle really acknowledged his frailty and humbled himself before God, he seems to have been all the more arrogant before men. Carlyle, who stressed that "Christianism was Humility, a nobler kind of Valour," was a person who had no humility in his intercourse with his fellow beings. Even Froude, who wrote a very sympathetic biography of Carlyle, acknowledged "Carlyle's extraordinary arrogance" and said that it was "a fault of which no one who knew Carlyle, or who has ever read his letters, can possibly acquit him."[36]

Uchimura, too, acknowledge Carlyle's personal faults, but defended him. "Carlyle was. . . a very narrow person. He did not receive many of his visitors. However, at the end his friend Emerson came to understand him. A true lover of mankind was not broadminded Emerson, but narrow Carlyle."[37] By choosing Carlyle as his mentor, Uchimura could justify and even exalt his own narrowness and could therefore accept himself. In an essay on "The Benefits of Narrowness" he quoted with approval the following statement. "Although they say that truth lies in the mean, it, in fact, lies in the extreme."[38] Uchimura criticized members of established denominations for their apparent devotion to tranquility and balance:

> Church Christians hate nothing so much as extremism. They love tranquility more than anything else. However, they do not know that Christianity itself is an extreme religion. . . Church Christians avoid narrowness more than anything else, and they love broadmindedness. However, they do not know that Christianity itself is a narrow religion.[39]

And he pointed to the anger of great men to justify his frequent loss of temper: "There are people who never get angry. However, such people are very dubious people. Carlyle got angry. Dante got angry. Paul got angry.

35. Zenshū, XIX, p. 143.
36. Carlyle, Heroes and Hero-Worship, p. 111; Froude, First Forty Years, II, p. 230.
37. Zenshū, X, p. 189.
38. Ibid., X, p. 188.
39. Ibid., XIII, p. 529.

Christ got angry. The teachers who have led me to the truth were all people who got angry."[40]

Because of his inability to get on with or to work with others, Uchimura was inevitably a lone wolf. He characteristically defended his isolation in "The Influence of a Single Man" by citing the examples of Carlyle and Tolstoi.

> A single Caryle has a greater influence than the entire Anglican Church upon the British people. A single Tolstoi has a greater influence on Russia and the whole world than the entire Russian Orthodox Church. We know from this that we have no need whatsoever to depend on churches and other organizations in our endeavour to lead people to goodness.[41]

When Uchimura was advised to "be courageous like Carlyle and gentle as St. Francis," he refused to be such an "hermaphrodite" and continued to see his mission in living "courageous like Carlyle," which meant not only in love but in hate. "Does the Christian or any religion prescribe love of scoundrels, then? I hope it prescribes a healthy hatred of scoundrels," wrote Carlyle. Uchimura expressed his hearty approval of this idea by drawing a line beside the passage and writing "Yea!" Like Carlyle, Uchimura felt "Love which does not know anger is a false love."[42]

The example of Carlyle helped to strengthen Uchimura's "rugged individualism." Uchimura stands out clearly in a society which tends to be group oriented, ready to submerge individual wills in the name of collective harmony. Since World War II, many Japanese have come to entertain grave doubts about the wisdom of group orientation. They deplore the stunted growth of individualism in Japan. To them Uchimura, who "refused" to bow before the Imperial signature, and opposed the popular Russo-Japanese War, appears to be an attractive example of healthy individualism. Herein lies a major reason for the strong postwar interest in Uchimura. Uchimura's individualism may indeed be attractive; but individualism cannot be developed by blindly imitating his example. Just as in the case of Carlyle, Uchimura's individualism at times verged on sheer egotism and conceit. Again like Carlyle, he did not know how to cooperate with and live in harmony with others instead of being surrounded by uncritical admirers. Yamaji Aizan,

40. Ibid., XIX, p. 805.
41. Ibid., XII, p. 503.
42. Ibid., XIII, p. 644; Carlyle, Latter-Day Pamphlets, p. 58.

perhaps the best contemporary critic of Uchimura, wrote addressing Uchimura:

> You are certainly one of the best contemporary writers. However, you are by no means a person who trained himself in intercourse with men. . . Your face has a kind of awe-inspiring dignity. Your conversation, however, betrays a kind of childishness. You have great self-confidence. It almost appears that, in your opinion, the entire world is drunk, and you alone are sober. However, are you really the only sober one and the entire world really drunk?. . . Your extreme distrust of others and your boundless confidence in yourself can never be said to be well-balanced.[43]

John Nichol concluded the biographical section of his Thomas Carlyle as follows:

> Hebraism, says Matthew Arnold, is the spirit which obeys the mandate, "walk by your light." Hellenism the spirit which remembers the other, "have a care your light be not darkness;" the former prefers doing to thinking, the latter is bent on finding the truth it loves. Carlyle is a Hebraist unrelieved and unretrieved by the Hellene. A man of inconsistencies, egotisms, Alpine grandeurs, and crevasses, let us take from him what the gods or protoplasms have allowed. His way of life, duly admired for its stern temperance, its rigidity of noble aim--eighty years spent in contempt of favour, plaudit, or regard, left him austere to frailty other than his own, and wrapt him in the repellent isolation which is the wrong side of uncompromising dignity. He was too great to be, in the common sense, conceited. All his consciousness of power left him with the feeling of Newton, "I am a child gathering shells on the shore": but what sense he had of fallibility arose from his glimpse of the infinite sea, never from any suspicion that, in any circumstances, he might be wrong and another mortal right.

Uchimura drew a line along the margin of this part (pp. 164-65) and wrote in big letters in Japanese: "All of this must be what people want to say about me." If we substitute Uchimura for Carlyle, this passage makes a pertinent comment on Uchimura.

43. "Waga mitaru Yaso kyōkai no shosensei, ina" Aizan Bunshū, ed. Uchiyama Shōzo (Minyūsha, 1917), pp. 940-41.

# SERVICE TO CHRIST AND COUNTRY: UCHIMURA'S SEARCH FOR MEANING

Robert Lee

With the collapse of the Tokugawa government that brought an end to 250 years of isolation, "the new generation in Meiji Japan"[1] suddenly found itself immersed in a flood of western ideas. This "new generation" encountered a new world view governed by the laws of science, and a new conception of society based upon the values of nationalism, both of which undermined the traditional Confucian world view and feudal social order that had for centuries provided the Japanese their self-identity. In short, the "new generation" faced a severe cultural identity crisis.[2]

This cultural identity crisis involved conflict on several levels: between intellectual and emotional modes of perception, and between the rhetoric of public debate and the agony of an inner search for personal meaning. Intellectually, the "new generation" repudiated the world view of their discredited past; however, emotionally they clung to the values of their former elite (samurai) social status. In public they debated the meaning of nationhood and the future of the Japanese state, but in private they agonized over their inability to define for themselves a significant role in the new state. Because they had publicly rejected their heritage, they could not return to Confucian or feudal categories to find meaning for their intense aspiration to become the new elite in a new social order. Nor could they easily adopt the new and more universal western values, which to them seemed to deny their extreme self-consciousness, derived from their samurai heritage, as the Japanese elite.

1. The phrase is taken from the title of a book by Kenneth B. Pyle and subtitled, Problems of Cultural Identity, 1885-1895, (Stanford University Press, 1969).
2. For further discussion of the "new generation," see Pyle, op. cit., pp. 6-22.

For many of the "new generation" a simple resolution of their cultural identity crisis became possible after Japan's dramatic victory in the Sino-Japanese war (1894-1895) that led to the recognition of Japan by the West as a powerful, modern nation-state.[3] However, for a few sensitive individuals the resolution of the meaning for nationhood in terms of an imperialistic Japanese nation-state was incompatible with the (normative) ideal of Japan that they had espoused from the beginning. Moreover, their personal identity crisis became even more severe as they discovered that neither a traditional nor a modern Japan offered them an opportunity to find personal meaning in the life of their nation. Withdrawal from society, a narcissistic inward turning to the self, or suicide became the fate of many of this latter group.[4]

Uchimura Kanzō (1861-1930) was one of the most sensitive of the "new generation." In modern Japanese history he became famous for his personal refusal to accept the Japanese nation-state as normative, a refusal that at the turn of the century led him to reject the course of the national polity. Some western historians see his new stance as a "failure" in political terms or as an "enigma" in personal terms.[5] Yet, in his own mind he remained all of his life a patriot in the service of both Christ and his country.

Since the end of World War II, to many Japanese Uchimura has become the representative hero of personal independence. Although once called a national traitor (lese majesty affair), in 1961 he was honored nationally in a centennial anniversary (one of the first Meiji-era figures so celebrated), which included the issuing of a special commemorative postage stamp. His writings are now included in Japanese high school textbooks. "Even on children's playing cards is written 'Kanzō Uchimura is the lighthouse of the mind.'"[6]

The purpose of this study is to show how Uchimura's agonizing, personal search for meaning could become paradigmatic for modern Japanese also in search of independence and integrity.[7] His extreme loyalty to transcendent

3. See Pyle on Tokutomi, op. cit., pp. 197-98.
4. Robert N. Bellah, "Ienaga Saburō and the Search for Meaning in Modern Japan," in Marius B. Jansen (ed.), Changing Japanese Attitudes toward Modernization, (Princeton University Press, 1965), p. 422.
5. Tatsuo Arima, The Failure of Freedom: A Portrait of Modern Japanese Intellectuals, Chapter 2, "Uchimura Kanzō: The Politics of Spiritual Despair," pp. 15-50; and John Forman Howes, "Japan's Enigma: The Young Uchimura Kanzō," unpublished Ph.D. dissertation, Columbia University, 1965.
6. Naoshi Koike, "Kanzō Uchimura: A Summary of His Life and Faith," Memoirs of the Muroran Institute of Technology, 5:2 (July, 1965).
7. Parts of this study I used earlier in, "The Individuation of the Self in Japanese History," Japanese Journal of Religious Study, 4:5-39 (March, 1977).

reality (Christ) provided him the basis for disinterested loyalty to empirical reality (Japan). In other words, loyalty to Christ provided him the independence and integrity to refuse to be compromised by the events of national history and to reject a strategy of withdrawal from society, either in terms of an other-worldly salvation or an inner-worldly turning to the self. Instead, loyalty to Christ drove him to service to both Christ and his country within the empirical reality of the nation-state.

## Samurai Christian

Like many of the "new generation," the traditional and the modern converged in Uchimura's early education. He was raised in a samurai, Confucian-oriented family; but he received his formal education in western-oriented schools. According to Uchimura:

> My father was a good Confucian scholar, who could repeat from memory almost every passage in the writings and sayings of the sage. So naturally my early education was in that line, and. . . I was imbued with the general sentiments of. . . loyalty to my feudal lords and fidelity and respect to my parents.[8]

However, Uchimura did not follow in his father's classical training; instead, he chose the new modern training in English language schools—a course that led him to the new government agricultural college in Sapporo, Hokkaido.[9] In college Uchimura, proud son of a samurai, converted to Christianity.

Historians have noted that all the outstanding early Christian converts had a common social background: all were not only from the samurai class, which lost its elite status in the Meiji Restoration, but were also from the domains that had not originally supported the Restoration and had consequently been excluded as a group from participation in the leadership of the Meiji government. These alienated elites sought to recover their lost social status

8. Uchimura Kanzō zenshū (The Complete Works of Uchimura Kanzō), XV, 10. (All references to the collected works of Uchimura are from the edition, edited by Suzuki Toshirō, Iwanami Shoten, Tokyo, 1932-33, and hereafter cited as Zenshū. All italics or emphasis are Uchimura's and all brackets are mine unless otherwise designated.)
9. The College was set up by William S. Clark, a former U.S. army officer, president of Massachusetts Agricultural College, graduate of Amherst College, and devout (Puritan) Christian.

and to fulfill their aspirations to leadership in society by converting to Christianity in order to acquire the western learning and techniques needed for modernizing Japan. These samurai converts easily embraced Christianity because the Protestant missionaries taught that Christian ethics underlay the progress and strength of western culture and because the samurai ethic was similar to the Christian ethic, especially as exemplified by the early Protestant (Puritan) missionaries. Hence the young samurai's conversion represented a transfer of loyalty from one's former lord (who was no longer viable in Meiji Japan) to a new Lord. In this way the young samurai Christian convert not only dealt with his personal identity crisis but also created for himself a new role in Japan's modernization that was independent of the oligarchic establishment of the original Meiji reformers.[10] Among these early samurai converts to Christianity (who made up 30% of the early Meiji Christians), Uchimura Kanzō became one of the most outstanding.

When Uchimura graduated in 1881 at the top of his class, he seemed poised at the beginning of a promising career of service to both Christ and country. He stayed in Sapporo to work in the government fishery department, a task that took him to all parts of Hokkaido to oversee the development of fish resources. Together with his Christian classmates he also established a tightly-knit fellowship of Sapporo Christians that grew so rapidly that they borrowed $400 from a Methodist missionary to build a church building.

From the beginning Uchimura and his friends envisioned a single, united church in Sapporo. Hence, the members who had been baptized earlier by two different missionaries into two different church denominations withdrew their denominational affiliation to establish a new, independent church in Sapporo. When the Methodist missionary, who had loaned the money for the new church building, learned of the disaffiliation of Uchimura's group from his denomination, he demanded immediate repayment of the money. Uchimura and his small band of "ten productive members"[11] responded with a strong reaffirmation to serve Christ in an independent, united church in Sapporo and with a pledge to repay the debt within a year, a pledge they fulfilled with great sacrifice. Uchimura never forgot this incident. It permanently shaped his negative attitude toward foreign missionaries and denominationalism and his determination to achieve both spiritual and financial independence.

10. This thesis has been argued most recently by Irwin Scheiner, Christian Converts and Social Protest in Meiji Japan (University of California Press, 1970), especially chapters 2, 3, and 4.
11. Zenshū, XX, p. 29.

**Direct or Indirect Ministry?**

Although the sudden demand to repay the $400 represented a heavy burden, it is clear from the many letters that Uchimura wrote to his closest friends that he was experiencing personal uncertainty and emotional anguish that was not directy related to the task of raising funds to repay this debt. These letters indicate that he found his official position in government service "loathsome, oppressive, unsatisfactory and corruptive." He felt that his superiors did "not know the utility of science" and did not fully utilize his talents and training. Above all Uchimura agonized over his future career of "how, when and WHERE will I be most useful both for Christ and for country," of whether his service should be "fishing on the sea" or "fishing of men," as "a fisherman of Hokkaido or a fisherman of Galilee."[12]

In a long letter to his close friend Miyabe Kingō, Uchimura asked, "How can I be most serviceable for the sake of God and mankind?" Rhetorically, first he considered a career of scientific research in biology as a way to show the compatibility of science and Christianity, especially by developing a theistic theory of evolution in order to oppose atheistic theories of evolution; but he finally rejected this course since his closest friend had advised him that he did not have the patient disposition for scientific research. Second, he considered continuing in the field of fishery science and returning to service in the government again, but he decided that this course would be a last resort only "to feed" himself and his family.[13] Third, he considered the ministry:

> Ministry?—No, I think. My too great nervousness, rough character, deficient eloquence, as well as weak sensibility forbid me to take this work as my life-service to the society. Moreover, my large family to be supported with my weak struggling health is a grand obstacle to this work.[14]

Discouraged about his future in Hokkaido, Uchimura resigned his government position and returned to his parental home in Tokyo to seek a new career. In Tokyo he finally decided to return to government service in the Fishery Section of the Ministry of Agriculture and Commerce, where he very productively turned out research monographs on the salmon, herring and cod and "the catalogue of Japanese fishes to be inserted in Dr. Chamberlain's New

12. Ibid., pp. 48, 60, 52 and 41.
13. Ibid., pp. 33, 78 ff. Miyabe, Uchimura's classmate at Sapporo, later became an outstanding biologist.
14. Ibid., p. 79.

Dictionary of Japanese and English."[15] He also sought out the fellowship of Tokyo Christians but found the Tokyo churches cold and indifferent. Finally, on a vacation he discovered the rural Annaka Church, which was "warm, affectionate, brotherly, and above all, active" like the Sapporo church, which he so missed.[16]

Uchimura here met and fell in love with Asada Take, a Christian of the Annaka Church, "a pretty, accomplished lady, sharp, though calm. . .of intromental temperament, who writes Japanese well, though poor in English." Eight months later after strong opposition from his parents, especially his mother, and after twice breaking off the engagement for the sake of filial piety, he obtained the reluctant consent of his parents and quickly married Take on March 28, 1884. Seven months later in October Take was sent back to her parents in Annaka. Uchimura was very vague about the reason for the divorce, saying only that she "was found to be a rascal—a wolf in sheep's skin." Severely criticized by the Christian community both for his sudden divorce and also for his adamant refusal even to consider a reconciliation, on November 4, 1884, he abruptly left for America to find relief.[17]

15. Ibid., p. 97.
16. Ibid., p. 74.
17. Ibid., pp. 97, 126-27. Uchimura's followers usually suggest that Take committed adultery and hence justify Uchimura's divorce on biblical grounds (Matt. 19:9). There is no real evidence to this claim. More likely the conflict of personalities between Uchimura's mother and her daughter-in-law disillusioned Uchimura, who later argued that "to the Japanese no relationship can be greater than the sacred relation of child to parent. Infidelity in this regard is, in Japan, synonomous with immorality" (in "Moral Traits of the Yamato-damashii ('Spirit of Japan')," Methodist Review, LXVIII-5th series, II:57 (Jan., 1886), Uchimura's italics). Thus the "immorality" that Uchimura saw was two-fold: his wife's because of her refusal to subordinate herself to her mother-in-law, and his own because he had gone against his mother's wishes in marrying Take. The latter especially grieved Uchimura since he felt he had defiled his family heritage and may explain his adamant refusal to consider reconciliation even though Take was pregnant with his child. For further discussion see Ohara Shin's critical biography of Uchimura (Hyōden Uchimura Kanzō, Tokyo, 1976), pp. 59-67. This fine study was not available to me before this paper was written.

**Flight to America**

Uchimura, as well as his two closest friends from Sapporo, Miyabe Kingō and Nitobe Inazō,[18] had always expected to go abroad to further his education, but the abruptness of his decision to leave for America caught him unprepared and undecided about what his future vocation should be, what advanced training he should seek and how he might finance such plans. Uchimura had time only to secure introductions through mutual friends to Dr. Isaac Kerlin, a Philadelphia Quaker and philanthropist, who often helped Japanese students. He had vague hopes that through Dr. Kerlin he might also finally enter medical school at the University of Pennsylvania or, if that was not possible, go to England for further study. Since Uchimura arrived in the United States in January, 1885, he had the first half of the year to decide more definitely about his future career and to make concrete plans for further education in the fall. Dr. Kerlin, who was in charge of a new institution for retarded children, provided Uchimura both a place to live and a place to work at his hospital, introduced him to many important people[19] who could offer him assistance in his future career; and with his wife treated him with warmth and kindness, experiences which in later years he recalled with great affection.

In spite of his new and warm social environment, Uchimura missed deeply the warm fellowship of the Sapporo Church, even though Nitobe, who had preceded him to the United States, was at nearby Johns Hopkins University. In his loneliness he turned inward--he studied science textbooks to prepare for medical school, continued his avid interest and reading of books on science and religion, and wrote long letters in English prose and poetry to close friends of his Sapporo days in which he expressed his longing for the companionship, affection, and approbation of his Sapporo friends.[20]

In his letter to Nitobe in the first half of 1885, Uchimura brooded continually over his "black past and wearisome future." As he neared his twenty-fifth birthday, he bemoaned his "wasted past," an "awful past, one

18. Miyabe and Nitobe and Uchimura were classmates in the foreign language school in Tokyo, attended college together, became Christians together, and formed the nucleus of the church in Sapporo.
19. Through Kerlin Uchimura also met President Cleveland. See Uchimura's letter of June 21, 1885, to Niishima, in Otis Cary, "Uchimura no ketsudan no natsu—1885" (The Summer of Uchimura's Decisive Decision—1885), _Jimbungaku_, 24 (1954), p. 99. (Cited hereafter as Cary, "Uchimura.")
20. _Zenshū_, XX, pp. 136-160.

continuous blank of failures and mistakes."[21] He felt both a deep shame for his "wasted past" and a heavy burden of guilt for his "black past," especially for his failure in marriage, a failure for which he condemned himself severely and yet protested his sincerity of intention:

> I feel much ashamed for my thoughtlessness in the selection of my wife; but I wish thee to pity me in this respect, for I did it because I thought it to be God's will. I have sinned to God, and to my parents and not less to thee. If to err is human, I am intensely so. Ah! those crazy hours, when I found one whom I called my "elder sister," and loved that sister more than my parents! O! those horrible times in Satan's devices, when I was a slave to my passionate love, which I mistook to be Divine! I wronged them (parents) very much by my last act, and I have to use my best possible means to please them.[22]

Uchimura realized that in his failure to meet the expectations of his parents, of the Christian community and especially—in his conscience—of God and of his dearest friends (Nitobe, in this case), he had hurt those whom he loved the most and from whom he most needed approbation. This hurt, as De Vos has shown,[23] produces an extreme sense of guilt, guilt that can lead to masochistic aggression upon one's own self, such as extreme self-criticism in

21. Zenshū, XX, pp. 144, 148, 152. Uchimura waxed poetic about his "wasted past": "My 25th birthday is at hand. A quarter of a century was wasted away. The agonized heart burst out in two stanzas:

Grass has grown and has wither'd
Twenty-five times, since from the womb,
This wretched vessel was launched
On its voyage toward the tomb

Like a tiny mountain stream
Running from some bitter source,
Not an herb has life derived
From its flow for half its course."

22. This quote is a composite of statements from Ibid., pp. 127, 138, 145 and 151. Uchimura's term "crazy" here has the connotation of "feeble-minded" and is a take-off from the heading of his letter, "'Home of Crazy Folks,' Elwyn, Pa." (Zenshū, XX, p. 144). Uchimura in his letters frequently used the term "crazy" non-pejoratively to refer to the feeble-minded children at Kerlin's hospital.

23. George De Vos, "The Relationship of Guilt toward Parents to Achievement and Arranged Marriage among the Japanese," Psychiatry, 23 (Aug., 1960), pp. 287-301. De Vos' point here is that in Japanese psychology guilt is related primarily to ego functions rather than to super-ego functions as in the west.

Uchimura's case, and also to powerful motivation for ascetic achievement in order to fulfill the expectations of the loved-hurt ones and thus to gain their approbation. According to De Vos, traditionally for Japanese:

> The only way open to the child (to deal with his guilt) is to attain the goal of highest value, which is required of him; by working hard, being virtuous, becoming successful, attaining a good reputation and the praise of society, he brings honor to himself, to his parents, and to his ie (household lineage), of which he and his parents are, after all, parts.[24]

In Uchimura's case, however, the process of the resolution of guilt became complicated because he had not only internalized the traditional (samurai) values of loyalty to the family heritage (ie) but also the Christian values of loyalty to Christ. As the eldest son and head of the family he felt a great responsibility toward his family--his aging parents and his younger brothers and sister. Earlier he had partially supported his family out of his ample stipends as a college student and his even larger salary as a government official, first in Hokkaido and then in Tokyo. Now in disgrace and nearly penniless, he could only wistfully hope to fulfill his obligations to his familiy:

> As to my domestic happiness, I have only one of caring (for) my parents in a nice comfortable house. I wronged them very much by my last act, and I have to use my best possible means to please them.[25]

Yet, Uchimura would also write: "If I should starve to death, I am satisfied to do so. I am willing to do anything if for the sake of Christ." "Promising future, only in Christ?"[26] Thus, in America Uchimura continued to agonize about his future, seeking a career in which he might fulfill both his role-obligations to his family and his duty to his new lord, Jesus Christ.

## Loyalty to Christ

The problem that Uchimura faced, in one sense, was a traditional one—a conflict of loyalties to one's own family (filial piety) and to one's lord. Ideally this conflict did not arise since the family and the lord were of the

24. Ibid., p. 293ff.
25. Zenshū, XX, p. 151.
26. Ibid., pp. 150, 144 ff.

same social order. As Uchimura put it: "in Japanese eyes filial love is the foundation stone of all virtues, loyalty to masters is the crown of them all."[27] However, when disruptions in the social order did allow conflicts to arise, in Japan loyalty to the lord superseded that to his parents. According to Uchimura:

> A man may leave his parents and follow his master, but he cannot do the opposite. "A loyal servant shall not have two masters under heaven." "Go ye and serve our master; let this old feeble soldier die alone," are the words with which an aged father sent forth his sons when their services were required by their master.[28]

Hence, for Uchimura loyalty to one's lord, which was central to the traditional samurai ethic, was also the highest virtue in the service to his new Lord. Such loyalty was the unconditional fulfillment of one's role-obligations—whether as son to his parents (filial piety), as servant to his lord, or even as lord to his servants—with sincerity and earnestness, without any expectation of recompense, and without any consideration of one's own life, safety or self-interest. In other words, loyalty required total self-dedication and self-sacrifice in order to _achieve_ one's given role in society. In his essay on the "Moral Traits of the _Yamato-damashii_ ('Spirit of Japan')," all of his illustrations described situations in which the hero at great sacrifice, including the giving of his own life, fulfilled his duties of fidelity or loyalty. Never did Uchimura reduce this loyalty to purity of motivation or intention; for him, loyalty always was inseparable from achievement.[29]

Uchimura saw this traditional samurai loyalty as an "inborn faculty" of the "Yamato-heart" already "essentially Christian _in spirit_," that is, in purity of motivation. In the past this loyalty had been blind, misdirected and even naive in its achievement, but now he asked rhetorically:

27. "Moral Traits of the _Yamato-damashii_ ('Spirit of Japan')," _Methodist Review_, LXVIII—5th series, II:61 (Jan., 1886). Uchimura wrote this essay in August, 1885, in order to defray expenses for his vacation at Gloucester, Mass. See his _Zenshū_, II, p. 865, for circumstances surrounding the writing of this essay. Also see John F. Howes, "Two Works by Uchimura Kanzō Until Recently Unknown in Japan," _Transactions of the International Conference of Orientalists in Japan_, III (1958), pp. 25-31.
28. "Moral Traits," p. 62 ff.
29. _Ibid._, p. 57.

> Is it a Utopian dream to hope that before a people like the Japanese pass through manifold experiences in the attainment of right government and wise administration they may enter, without further preparation, that free kingdom where their inborn faculties will be accepted just as they are, and consecrated to labor in higher, holier spheres? Have not the olden traditions of loyalty to a chief. . .prepared them (samurai Japanese) in a certain degree for the simple fidelity which should exist among the sharers in that realm where he that will "be the chiefest shall be servant of all?"[30]

Thus Uchimura believed that samurai loyalty was not only "essentially Christian" in its motivation, but that when consecrated and redirected to service to Christ, it was the first and prior step to service to country, to the "attainment of right government and wise administration."

However, for Uchimura loyalty to Christ was also different from all traditional loyalties of the samurai ethic. Even though loyalty to Christ involved the same purity of motivation as the traditional samurai loyalty, its orientation for achievement was found not within the traditional social order of family, society and nation but in a transcendent order. Hence, loyalty to Christ required not only a surrender of the self to Christ (disinterested loyalty) but also a total self-dedication to the fulfillment of the "will of God," that is, to loyal actions that denied absolute value to family, society and nation. Thus Uchimura's loyalty to Christ both freed him from the ascribed role-obligations of his social order and provided him a new identity in Christ, a self-identity now independent of the social order. In other words, Uchimura's loyalty to Christ did not diminish his samurai spirit of self-denial and self-dedication but set these motivations and actions in a higher or transcendent context from which he could critically judge the nature of his loyalty (to Christ) both in his actions in his roles in the family, society, and nation, and in his motivations and aspirations in fulfilling these human roles in society. In short, in his loyalty to Christ Uchimura acquired an extremely sensitive conscience which in future years set him apart from his own countrymen.[31]

30. Ibid., p. 66 ff. The passage quoted by Uchimura is from Mark 10:44 (KJV).
31. In De Vos' psychological language Uchimura's guilt-loyalty syndrome ("I have sinned to God—loyalty to Christ") acquired super-ego functions in addition to the traditional ego functions. See note 23 above.

## Again—Direct or Indirect Ministry?

Because of his total loyalty to Christ, Uchimura agonized much over the decision that faced him at the beginning of the summer of 1885. After six months with the Kerlins in Elwyn (a suburb of Philadelphia) he still had not decided upon the direction of his future and could not make concrete plans for his education in the fall. When the Kerlins initiated arrangements, including a promise of $300 a year, for him to enter the medical school of the University of Pennsylvania, Uchimura seemed delighted: the study of medicine would enable him to continue his longstanding personal interest in biology, it would be helpful in his service to Christ and man, and it would provide a means to become financially independent of the "aid of government or private societies" as well as a means to support his family in comfort.[32] In the meantime, he met with Niishima Jō, who was on a tour of the United States and had learned from Nitobe in Baltimore that Uchimura was "very gloomy, & does not know what to do."[33] Niishima, an Amherst College Graduate (1870), offered to help him enter Amherst College. Uchimura was again delighted: "My spirit longs after Amherst, there to pursue the study I took up a few years ago, viz. the interpretation of the Bible by the Biological and Geological facts."[34] However, he continued to agonize:

> . . . though my friends scorn me for my indecision, "mine eyes are pouring tears toward God." Direct or indirect ministries are still perplexing questions to me. If the former is God's will, I must be placed under the care of such saints as Dr. Seelye (president of Amherst College), but if the latter is what I should do, I wish to be a healer of flesh.[35]

As he faced again the question of the "direct" or "indirect ministry," Uchimura deliberately intensified the inner conflict in order to discover the "will of God." He asked himself if his interest in the "direct ministry" was because of the voice of God or because of "the nobility of the work of the

32. Letter to Niishima, June 21, 885; and Niishima's journal notes of May 7 and 8, in Cary, "Uchimura," pp. 101, 130. Niishima Jō, or Joseph Hardy Neesima as he was also known, was the first Japanese graduate of a western institution of higher learning (Amherst College) and founder of Dōshisha University in Kyoto.
33. Letter to Niishima, June 2, 1885, in Otis Cary, "Uchimura, Neesima and Amherst—Recently Discovered Correspondence," Japan Quarterly, III (1956) p. 447 (Hereafter cited as Cary, "Correspondence.").
34. Letter to Niishima, June 27, 1885, in Cary, "Uchimura," p. 107.
35. Zenshū, XX, p. 157.

ministry over other occupations."[36] Was his decision for the "direct ministry" one of loyalty to Christ or one of pride, the seeking of the approbation of the Christian community in whose eyes he was disgraced? He was well aware that in the past his most well-intended obedience had proved blind and disastrous. Hence, he agonized over discerning God's will: how could one know what was God's will; how did one "distinguish between true and false inspiration," between inspiration and "fanatism (sic) and insanity that passed under the name of inspiration?"[37] He resignedly concluded:

> God only knows whether it (inspiration) be true or not, and as for man, it only remains to test it by his conscience and reasonings as much as he can, and follow a conviction which has the greatest weight. If he makes a mistake after these precautions, he "can't be helped," because he cannot go any further.[38]

For Uchimura this painful process of the inner conflict of a reasoning conscience, testing every "inspiration" (or motivation and aspiration), was an intrinsic element in his loyalty to Christ. Far from despising his agonizing search for the will of God, he wrote: "Submission, resignation, and sanctification are the sweetest results of well regulated trials."[39] Although Uchimura's statement contained terms filled with western theological content, the meaning of his statement can be better understood as an expression of his samurai loyalty to Christ—"submission" was loyal obedience to one's lord; "resignation" was a disinterested loyalty tested by conscience; and "sanctification" was the self-dedication to the fulfillment of the will of one's lord.

By the end of July he was both emotionally and physically near collapse, exhausted by his inner struggles. Upon the advice of Niishima, Uchimura, who felt bound to the Kerlins "by their too much kindness," left the Kerlins "peacefully" to go to Gloucester, Massachusetts, in order to recuperate in a new and more neutral environment.[40] Niishima admonished him not to engage "in ascetic meditation" but simply to "lay yourself at the foot of the Cross & wait for his further Guidance." He again suggested: "Why can't you come to Amherst & spend <u>a year or two</u> before you take your professional study."[41] In August Uchimura replied to Niishima from Gloucester:

36. <u>Ibid.</u>, p. 158.
37. <u>Ibid.</u>, p. 158 ff.
38. Letter to Niishima, June 2, 1885, in Cary, "Correspondence," p. 447.
39. Letter to Niishima, July 5-6, 1885, in Cary "Uchimura," p. 111.
40. Draft of letter from Niishima to Uchimura, n.d., in Cary, "Uchimura," p. 117.
41. <u>Ibid.</u>, emphasis mine.

> Having cast all my cares upon God, I have nothing to say about my own future. I intend to go to Amherst, awaiting your kind concern, and to fulfill my long intention to be a minister of the Gospel.[42]

Thus in September he entered Amherst College as a special student in the junior class.

At Amherst Uchimura's spirit could not find rest. At times his spirit soared as he exulted over his studies in science, history and Bible:

> I rejoice to know that nature, History, and the Bible are the tripod of God's revelation to mankind. . . To find out _spiritual_ in _natural_; O, what a pure joy and pleasure.[43]

At other times he had Job-like depressions:

> Today is my 2nd anniversary of my departure from Japan. . . For the past two years God has tried me in this strange land in various ways. I cried unto Him, but He has not answered. He took away from me all that I considered dear and precious unto me in this world. My friends scorned me when I was stricken by the Lord. I often have thought during the darkest and gloomiest hours that God was pursuing this poor worm to death.[44]

Nevertheless, after two years he was graduated from Amherst College, quite pleased with his credentials for his future career:

> I value the title (Bachelor of Science) very highly inasmuch as it was conferred without any intention on my part to receive. I think _nōgakushi ken rigakushi_ (Bachelor of Agriculture) and Bachelor of Science sound very good for a clergyman.[45]

In order "to become a good intelligent clergyman," in the fall Uchimura entered Hartford Theological Seminary; however, in February, 1888, he announced, "I have studied long enough" and abruptly left the Seminary in order to return to Japan.[46]

42. Letter to Niishima, Aug. 10, 1885, in Cary, "Uchimura," p. 125.
43. _Zenshū_, XX, p. 173.
44. _Ibid._, p. 175.
45. _Ibid._, p. 184 ff.
46. _Ibid._, pp. 186, 188.

What had caused this sudden move? Even though on the seacoast at Gloucester he had written Niishima that "the greatest burden of my soul was cast into the bay of Gloucester never to be even looked at" and that he was "perfectly happy," even "ready to die,"[47] he realized that his going to Amherst and later to Hartford was in fact another interlude, a further postponement of the actualization of his loyalty to Christ. Practically speaking, for Uchimura going to Amherst College simply put off the vocational or "professional" question for "a year or two." Niishima's counsel to him to study at Amherst had the effect of freeing him from his dependence on the Kerlins—that is, from the more liberal, urbane Philadelphia influence—and entrusting him into the hands of Julius Seelye, President of Amherst college and Niishima's former teacher—that is, to the more rural, Puritan influence of New England. But Uchimura could find rest neither at Amherst nor in the seminary at Hartford because his samurai-like loyalty to Christ could not be divided into a cognitive decision and an anticipated future action, but rather demanded from him the fulfillment of his loyalty in active service to Christ and country. For these reasons he returned to Japan in the spring of 1888.

## Return and Despair in Japan

Uchimura, a Japanese samurai Christian with degrees not only from a Japanese college, but also from an American college, seemed poised once more on the verge of a significant career, his second opportunity to fulfill his loyalty to Christ in active service to both Christ and country; however, he was again confronted by a series of setbacks. In the fall of 1888, as his first employment after his return to Japan, he accepted the appointment of the presidency of a new college in Niigata. He wrote to his friend, David Bell, with great expectation:

> I am going to superintend a school (they call it a college!) run wholly by the natives most of whom are non-Christians, but who desire to entrust the management of the school to a Christian superintendent. It is the first experiment of the kind in Japan—not a college run by the Govenment neither by an mission, but wholly by natives. You know, my principle is <u>Christo-national</u>, and any institution in my country which is not Christian and at

47. Letter to Niishima, Aug. 22, 1885, in Cary, "Uchimura," p. 128.

> the same time which is not national has but very little of my sympathy.[48]

Four months later because of serious conflict with volunteer (American Board) missionary-teachers over his understanding of Christianity and his approach to teaching it, he resigned when the school board sided with the missionaries and thus compromised his independence.

In the fall of 1890, after a year of illness and part-time employment, he became an instructor of history and English in the prestigious First Higher Middle School of Tokyo. Uchimura, writing to Bell, considered his "chief work" to be "the care of dormitories," "a kind of spiritual supervision" of "600 of the cleverest, sharpest, and wittiest of young sons of Japan."[49] However,

> On the 9th of Jan. there was in the High Middle School where I taught, a ceremony to acknowledge the Imperial Precept on Education. After the address of the President and reading of the said Precept, the professors and students were asked to go up to the platform one by one, and bow to the Imperial signature affixed to the Precept, in the manner as we used to bow before our ancestral relics as prescribed in Buddhist and Shinto ceremonies. I was not at all prepared to meet such a strange ceremony, for the thing was the new invention of the president of the school. As I was third in turn to go up and bow, I had scarcely time to think upon the matter. So, hesitating in doubt, I took a safer course for my Christian conscience, and in the august presence of sixty professors (all non-Christians, the two other Xtian prof.'s beside myself having absented themselves) and over one thousand students, I took my stand and did not bow! It was an awful moment for me, for I instantly apprehended the result of my conduct.[50]

What Uchimura actually did was to bow his head slightly toward the special copy of the Imperial Rescript of Education with the emperor's "signature" instead of bowing deeply (ninety degrees) from the waist. He had

48. Zenshū, XX, p. 191. Uchimura met David Bell, a businessman, through Isaac Kerlin. Although their acquaintance was very brief in the United States, Uchimura found a senior friend in whom he could confide. His 184 letters written to Bell, collected in volume XX of the Zenshū, remain the best source for understanding this period of Uchimura's life.
49. Ibid., p. 200.
50. Ibid., p. 206 ff. Uchimura's interpretation of the January 9th event (written March 6th) perhaps overdramatizes the actual event.

intended his bow to be like a normal act of courtesy, in this instance, a bow of respect for the emperor. His conscience prevented him from making the deeper bow since such an act of before a ribbon-bedecked piece of cardboard could be easily misconstrued as an act of worship, such as done before "ancestral relics." However, what Uchimura had intended to be a simple act of courtesy became instead an act of lese majesty.[51] He was accused of insulting "the nation's Head," desecrating the school and being a traitor to the nation. Although Uchimura protested in vain "that the good Emperor must have given the precepts to his subjects not to be bowed unto, but to be obeyed," and that he surely was faultless in his obedience "to the Imperial Precept in his daily conduct in the school," "the anti-Christian sentiments still strong in the school" made this minor incident a major event in the newspapers in order to attack "the Christians in general," to discredit them by questioning their loyalty to "the nation and its Head."[52]

In the meantime, when he was assured that to bow deeply was "to conform to the custom of the nation," and that the bow does not mean worship, but merely respect to the Emperor, he consented to the deep bow. Uchimura explained:

> That the bow does not mean worship, I myself have granted for many years. . . It was not refusal but hesitation and conscientious scruples which caused me to deny the bow at that moment; and now that the Principal assured me that it was not worship, my scruples were removed, and though I believe the ceremony to be a foolish one, for the sake of the school, the principal, and my students, I consented to bow.[53]

All this came too late. Seriously ill with influenza, he resigned his position in the school.

This series of setbacks immediately after his return from America nearly destroyed Uchimura both spiritually and physically. Not only had he been rebuffed in his first two attempts to serve Christ and country as a teacher, first in a private school and then in a government school, but also he had become anathema in the eyes of both the missionaries and his own

51. For a full discussion, see Ozawa Saburō, Uchimura Kanzō fukei jiken (The Lese Majesty Incident of Uchimura Kanzō). See also Ohara, Hyōden Uchimura Kanzō, pp. 116-137.
52. Zenshū, XX, p. 207 ff.
53. Ibid., pp. 208-9.

countrymen. In addition, his health seriously deteriorated during two long periods of illness, first from typhoid fever and then from pneumonia. Further, Uchimura's new wife, who faithfully nursed him back to health, came down with the same illness (pneumonia) and died. In despair, he cried:

> I read the book of Job over and over again, but I stop at Chap. XXX, 16-31 and read no further. Eli, Eli lame sabachthani![54] Art thou not, or was my faith in thee mistaken? I looked for light, and behold darkness! . . .Yes, before God I am an inexcusable sinner, and what punishments I deserve not. Yet shall a father strike his child when the latter sacrificed all to confess the former before the world? Yes, once He crucified His beloved Son, the most dutiful Son the world ever saw.[55]

Uchimura had indeed reached the low point in his life. In his loyalty to Christ and his conscience he had expected to be a Christian samurai in the service of his new Lord in a new Japan. However, his loyalty and conscience led him not into service in Japanese society but great disapprobation--accusations of betraying the nation, insulting the emperor and desecrating his school. Hopelessly, he wrote to his senior friend Bell:

> Ever since I refused to bow my head before the Imperial Signature, I have been an outcast from the Japanese society, all doors of usefulness except within a very narrow Christian circle being shut up against me. I often have thought of quitting my country, and to go either to Hawaii or to U.S. to spend the rest of my life.[56]

## Search for Meaning

Although Uchimura knew that he had failed to live up to the expectations of a man of his training and talent, he could not forsake the nation that he so loved—even though that nation had rejected him. Hence, he turned to writing a series of books and articles (that would make him famous again in the future), as well as to taking occasional teaching jobs in order to eke out a subsistence for his family. Perhaps an even deeper motivation for turning to

54. Uchimura cites a passage on extreme human suffering in the book of Job and then quotes the words of Jesus on the cross (Matthew 27:46 KJV).
55. Zenshū, XX, 214.
56. Ibid., p. 277 ff.

writing than earning a living was his need to explore again the question of what loyalty to Christ meant and especially how this loyalty might find actualization in concrete service. In his writings he sought to justify the pain and sufferings of his loyalty[57] and to depict the ideal Japan in which the services of a loyal samurai Christian wuld be most needed. In this latter vision he shared with his western-oriented contemporaries the belief in progress (Spencer) and the great man (Carlyle) as the logical extension of the samurai ideal of achievement of ends (progress) and of the superior (great) man.[58] As a Puritan Christian Uchimura extended this modernized samurai ideal even further with the idea of divine providence. For him divine providence meant that "men in all times, especialy great men" were appointed to specific tasks to a specific people at a specific time in history. Furthermore,

> If mankind in general has a definite end and aim, and if each individual is destined for a specific work in his time and place, then a nation, as a unit which goes to compose the whole human family, must have a work peculiar to itself, and contributory to the welfare and progress of the whole.[59]

Uchimura surely understood himself to be one of those "great men" divinely appointed "for a specific work in his time and place;" but before he could fulfill his destiny, he needed to understand Japan's place in divine providence:

> What is Japan's mission, or what can she do for the world? If Egypt and Babylon started civilization, Phoenicia dispersed it, Judea purified it, Greece polished it, Italy preserved it, Germany reformed it, England tempered it, and America executed it, is nothing more left for Japan to work upon?[60]

57. Among Uchimura's earliest writings (1893), Kirisuto Shinto no nagusame (Consolations of a Christian), in Zenshū, I, pp. 1-77; Kyuanroku (Search After Peace), in Zenshū, I, pp. 79-256, deal with the problems of loyalty to Christ—the former with the sufferings and the consolations of that loyalty, and the latter with the search for that disinterested loyalty. These two books are autobiographical and take up some of the events in Uchimura's life discussed earlier.
58. For a discussion of Japanese attitudes toward modernization during the first three decades of the Meiji era, see Marius B. Jansen, "Changing Japanese Attitudes Toward Modernization," in Changing Japanese Attitudes Toward Modernization, ed., Marius B. Jansen.
59. Zenshū, IVI, p. 16.
60. Ibid., p. 17.

Uchimura's response to the question of Japan's place in modern world was shaped by his wide reading of western history and especially the works of the cultural geographers, Carl Ritter (1779-1859) and his student, Arnold Guyot (1807-1884).[61] Following Ritter and Guyot, he argued that "two elements go to form a nation: land and people," that is, the geographical features and the ethnic characteristics of a nation, both set in the context of the course of world history. According to Uchimura, geographically:

> Japan stretches one arm toward America, now enjoying the choicest fruits of European civilization. On the other hand, she stretches the other arm towards the responding arms of Korea and China, the whole making Japan a steppingstone, as it were, between the Occidental and the Oriental continents. . . There she stands as an arbiter, a "middle man" (nakōdo) between the Democratic West and the Imperial East, between the Christian America and the Buddhist Asia.[62]

Ethnically (for Uchimura, the mental traits):

> The Japanese alone of all Oriental peoples can comprehend the Occidental ideas, and they alone of all civilized peoples have a true conception of Oriental ideas.[63]

Uchimura argued that historically western civilization marched from the (middle) east to the west, "through Babylon, Phoenicia, Greece, Rome, Germany, England, and culminated on the Pacific side of America." Further, "the law of the westward march was not reversed," but, western civilization reached Japan, which "within the past thirty years swallowed everything that Europe had to give us, and digestion (is) going on briskly now." Finally, eastern civilization, which also began in the middle east, "traveled through India, Thibet, and China" and reached Japan, which "imbibed the best of Korea, China and India, and the assimilation (was) well nigh complete." Hence, he concluded that the mission to which Japan was called to fulfill was "to reconcile the East with the West; to be the advocate of the East and the harbinger of the West."[64]

61. Guyot's book, The Earth and Man: Lectures on Comparative Physical Geography in its Relation to the History of Mankind (1894), very much shaped Uchimura's argument here and was the model and title for his later book, Chinjinron (1884), in Zenshū, I, pp. 531-653.
62. Zenshū, XVI, pp. 17, 20 ff.
63. Ibid., p. 21.
64. Ibid., p. 23 ff.

Uchimura's uncritical love for his nation became even more particularistic when he wrote in 1894, "Justification of the Corean War," an essay he later regretted writing. But in 1894, he argued:

> There was a time in World History when mankind went to war with no meaner motive than to establish Righteousness upon the face of the Earth. . . We believe that the Corean War was opened between Japan and China to be such a war—I mean, a righteous war. Righteousness we say, not only in a legal sense. . . but righteousness in moral sense as well—the only kind of righteousness that can justify any war.[65]

Thus Uchimura in his understanding of divine providence attributed to Japan a "divine humanity" with "a nobler motive than love of gain and empty honor when it goes into war."[66] The attribution was surely borrowed from his samurai ethic, but the arguments presented to support this ethic in 1894 were borrowed from western history, including biblical history.

As indicated above, Uchimura was later to regret writing his essay on the justification of the Sino-Japanese War of 1894-1895. Ostensibly the war was fought to gain the independence of Korea from Chinese suzerainty and thus to free Korea from imperialism and to open her to the benefits of modernization from the west (Japan). Instead, at the end of the war the Japanese not only secured Korea's independence from China but also

> obliged China to cede Formosa, the Pescadores, and the Liaotung (South Manchuria) Peninsula to Japan. . . pay two hundred million taels indemnity; open more ports (in China); and negotiate a commercial treaty. . . which gave Japan all the privileges that the Western powers had in China and added the further privilege of carrying on "industries and manufactures" using cheap labor, paid in depreciated silver, in the treaty ports.[67]

Therefore, Uchimura at the end of the war wrote to Bell in extreme embarrassment:

> A "righteous war" has changed into a piratic war somewhat and a prophet who wrote its "justification" is now in shame.[68]

65. Ibid., p. 27 ff.
66. Ibid., p. 27.
67. John K. Fairbank, Edwin O. Reischauer, and Albert M. Craig, East Asia: The Modern Transformation (Houghton Mifflin, 1965), p. 383 ff.
68. Zenshū, XX, p. 289.

Deeply disappointed by the military, political and economic aggrandizement of his nation against China, Uchimura turned to popular journalistic writing and with a sharp satirical pen attacked the national leadership. He juxtaposed the "Spirit of Yamato" incarnated in the samurai heroes of the past—men of sincerity, honesty, fidelity and righteousness—and the leading members of the nation-state whom he named: "Fukuzawa-Mammonism, Higo-Hypocrisy, Satsuma-Covetousness, and Chōshū-Insincerity."[69] Such journalistic writing also suddenly thrust Uchimura into fame and popularity. His uncompromising independence and loyalty to principle along with his grand style of satire, irony and wit established him as a "prophet," a moral, social and political critic of the Meiji establishment.

Uchimura's fame and popularity also landed him a prized post as a regular columnist on the Yorozu Chōhō, a flourishing, anti-establishment, socialist-oriented daily newspaper. Then, in 1903 war with Russia became imminent. This time, because of the broad popular appeal of the coming war, the formerly anti-government owner of the Yorozu Chōhō chose to back the government on the issue of war with Russia. Uchimura, who could not in good conscience support such a war, especially after his humiliating experience of supporting the earlier Sino-Japanese war, resigned from the staff of the newspaper.

## The Mature Uchimura

From the perspective of the general public Uchimura's dramatic resignation was a courageous act of conscience, a sacrifice of personal gain by a man of uncompromising principles. For Uchimura, however, this resignation was not one more disappointing setback which again aborted a promising career but, rather, the occasion to announce publicly a fundamental change in priorities and strategy in his service to Christ and country, a change which he had already privately initiated and one that was more consistent with his own aspirations from the beginning.

The necessity for this shift in direction became increasingly clear to Uchimura when he saw that Japan's rapid process of nation-building was acquiring the worst features of western civilization. Japan was trading away

69. For Uchimura's attack on Fukuzawa and the Meiji oligarchs, see Zenshū, XVI, pp. 131, 132, 140, 141, 148, 149.

its old samurai heritage—which for Uchimura was but one step away from true Christianity—for the decadence of the west, especially its materialism ("mammonism") and its policy of military and economic aggrandizement ("imperialism"). According to Uchimura, "under the Satsuma-Chōshū government" Japan had become an "immoral nation" and "a dead corpse."[70]

Because earlier he had gone so far as to attribute a special destiny in God's providence to the Japanese nation—a "divine humanity" with "a nobler motive than love of gain and empty honor,"[71] now after the events of 1895 and 1903 Uchimura was forced to rethink his optimistic view of history and divine providence. He concluded more pessimistically that the history of nations—whether those of western or eastern civilizations—could not be identified with the history of the "divine humanity":

> No less an authority than Spengler says that the Western civilization is already a decadent civilization doomed to die in the near future. As for the Eastern civilization, we know it to be an already dead civilization, a thing of the past, buried in the valley of the Ganges or on the banks of the Hoang-ho. Can a happy home be made by the marriage of a half dead man and an already dead woman?[72]

Although the events of history forced Uchimura to judge his nation as "immoral" and "dead," his love of country could not allow him to abandon his people. Instead, he differentiated between the Japanese as a nation and as "man," and described the latter as "a spiritual being, one that can rise above itself."[73] Hence, the most urgent priority was no longer nation-building, such as wars of expansion in the name of independence for Korea, but a revival of traditional personal morality: "Let Japanese sincerity reassert itself and there is yet hope for the establishment of the nation."[74] Henceforth, he would redirect his strategy of service from that of building a Japanese civilization to bridge East and West to that of building a new civilization of moral (spiritual) men and women. The latter, for Uchimura, was an old, yet new civilization that had been announced "twenty-six centuries ago (by) a Jew by the name of Isaiah," "given to us (in the sermon) on the mount," and "has been

70. Zenshū, XV, p. 576.
71. Zenshū, XVI, p. 27.
72. Zenshū, XI, p. 569.
73. Ibid., p. 572.
74. Ibid., p. 576.

handed down in the book which Christendom has professed to accept as the veritable Word of God, but has never tried to make it an actuality."[75]

This failure of moral civilization to become a reality in Japan as well as in the West also required Uchimura to consider a more radically transcendent view of divine providence, a view which his senior American friend, David Bell, advocated by his sending to Uchimura books and articles on the premillennial view of the second coming of Christ.[76] According to this view, the promised new civilization of the prophet Isaiah, of Jesus "on the mount," and of the Bible has been postponed until the second advent of Christ when "the Lord Himself will come down again to <u>convert</u> the world,"[77] and thus usher in the millennium, the thousand year reign of Christ on earth. At that time the Lord shall judge the nations:

> And He shall judge between the nations
> and shall decide for many peoples;
> And they shall beat their swords into plowshares,
> and their spears into pruning hooks;
> Nation shall not lift up sword against nation,
> neither shall they learn war anymore.[78]

Uchimura found great comfort in this apocalyptic notion of a divine intervention into world history in which "the Lord Himself. . . will. . . convert the world." This notion of divine providence not only enabled him to transcend all the incongruities in his own personal life and in his world, but also to accept them in all their ambiguities without either legitimizing or ignoring them. The premillennial view of history explained to him why "His elect. . . must suffer" until Christ returned. Until His return, loyalty to Christ required one to be "ready" and to be "a witness for him. . . amidst continual buffeting and revilings from (his) countrymen."[79] Thus, Uchimura could be "in the world but not of the world."

In a sense, Uchimura knew from the beginning of his brief but unsuccessful journalistic career that he was marking time, that this period was another interlude in his search for a viable career to fulfill his loyalty to Christ. Rather than blind loyalty that in the past had led to fruitless service

75. <u>Ibid.</u>, p. 570.
76. <u>Zenshū</u>, XX, p. 277 ff.
77. <u>Ibid.</u>, p. 277.
78. <u>Zenshū</u>, XV, p. 571. Uchimura quoted here Isaiah 2:4 and 11:6-11 (KJV).
79. <u>Zenshū</u>, XX, p. 278.

to Christ and country, Uchimura had matured in faith; he had learned to wait and even to suffer patiently, finding his only consolation in his trust in God. He knew that his service was to witness—the "direct ministry"—but he awaited the appropriate moment and occasion. At the beginning of his greatest popularity in 1897, he wrote to Bell:

> I often think I should go to direct preaching of the Gospel at once; but my services seem to be much required in editorial works, at least for the present. I humbly wait for the voice that shall command me to leave the net and go to the fishing of men. God knows, I am ready.[80]

## An Independent Ministry

Uchimura had sought from the time he finished college at Sapporo this opportunity to serve full time in the "direct ministry." His bitter experiences with missionary societies and denominationalism in the past had convinced him that involvement in the institutional church would inevitably lead to the compromising of his independence. Hence, he wanted a ministry that was both spiritually and financially independent of both foreign missionaries and their denominational churches:

> I shall never work under any missionary society. In a sense, I have a gospel peculiar to myself; and if ever I shall be a minister, I shall stand alone, standing upon God, and upon nothing else.[81]

In the years before 1903, Uchimura had gradually been developing on a marginal basis a program of "direct ministry" that would make him an "independent missionary." Because of the centrality of the Bible in his own life and the absence of "popular commentaries upon the Bible,"[82] in 1900 he began publishing his own magazine, Seisho no kenkyū (The Biblical Studies), a monthly magazine devoted to the simple exposition of the Bible and the Christian life. The magazine was a success from its beginning and went through 350 issues (1900-1930), reaching 4500 paid subscriptions. His writings thus provided him with a constituency to whom he became a traveling evangelist

80. Ibid., p. 345.
81. Ibid., pp. 345 ff.
82. Ibid., p. 251.

and Bible lecturer. In addition, he experimented with Sunday Schools and short-term Bible schools in his home and elsewhere. In 1901 he reported to Bell about the success of his monthly magazine and his new (part-time) role in the service of Christ and country.

> I traveled about 2000 miles this autumn, preaching the Gospel to my countrymen. My "heathen" countrymen hear me gladly, they paying all my expenses, and sometimes even paying me for my actual Christian service. The ideal of my youth is now partially realized. I am an independent missionary, the privilege, which indeed, very few men have either in Japan or in any country.[83]

By 1903, when once more because of conscience he was forced to terminate abruptly his career in journalism, Uchimura was indeed "ready" to leave "the nets to go fishing for men."

For the next twenty-five years Uchimura was involved in the most active ministry. In addition to editing and writing for his monthly magazine, Seisho no kenkyū, he regularly taught and preached on biblical topics in rented halls. His regular Sunday afternoon classes attracted audiences of 600-800 persons and sometimes reached over a thousand persons. When the hall that he rented burned down in the 1923 earthquake, his followers built him a new lecture hall beside his own house, where he preached and taught in two services every Sunday morning and evening in order to accomodate his followers in the smaller hall (capacity about 300-350 persons).[84]

The success of Uchimura's "direct ministry" led to a large following, a constituency for whom he was the sensei or spiritual leader, but one that he refused to organize. Periodically he disbanded his smaller and more intimate bible groups and gave specific instructions to disband his larger Sunday group and his magazine upon his death. Moreover, he encouraged his most mature followers to begin their own Bible study groups and magazines. As a consequence many other small bible study groups were organized, following the example and practice of Uchimura. Even in later years when these small groups proliferated (to as many as 50,000 adherents—a figure based upon the number of subscribers to the numerous Uchimura-type Bible study magazines) and became a national movement, they developed no infra-structure, formal relations or membership lists on a national or local level. Leadership in the groups, following the example of Uchimura, remained charismatic and based

83. Ibid., p. 372.
84. Koike, op. cit., p. 14.

upon the individual's personal integrity, independent of both the foreign missionaries and the denominational churches, did create an independent Christian movement in Japan which he called both "Christianity without church" (mukyōkaishugi kirisutokyō) and a "Japanese Christianity."

By mukyōkaishugi kirisutokyō Uchimura meant a Christianity based upon the principle of "no church" (or "non-church"). According to Uchimura, mukyōkai Christianity was not a negative phenomenon in opposition to the missionary-sponsored churches but rather:

> "No-church" is the church for those who have no church. . . In heaven there is no such thing as the church. As it is written in Revelation 21:22a, "I saw no temple (church) in the city (heaven)."
>
> However, while in this world we do need a church of this world. Hence some men join churches built by the hands of men, and there they praise God and receive His teaching. . . However, some of us are not members of such churches. . . What is our church and where is it?
>
> The universe which God created, that is, nature—this is the church in this world for us no-church Christian believers. . . No-church is the church. Only those who are without church in reality have the best [true] church.[85]

For Uchimura Christianity could not be confined to the limits of the institutional church because Christianity was a transcendent or universal religion, independent of particular historical realities. It was also independent of any national culture—whether that of western or eastern civilization; and it was independent of all political and social structures--whether they be national or ecclesiastical. However such a transcendent or universal religion was not an other-worldy experience, but a religion to be actualized in this world, since Uchimura was above all a samurai Christian and sought a Christianity engrafted on the "Spirit of Yamato"—a "Japanese Christianity":

> When a Japanese truly and independently believes in Christ, he is a Japanese Christian, and his Christianity is Japanese Christianity. . . A Japanese by becoming a Christian does not cease to be a Japanese. On the contrary, he becomes more Japanese by becoming a Christian. A Japanese who becomes an

85. Zenshū, IX, pp. 211-213. Parenthesis his, brackets and emphasis mine.

American or an Englishman or an amorphous universal man, is neither a true Japanese nor a true Christian.

Does Christianity lose by bringing the spirit of samurai into it? Was not Latin Christianity a happy fusion of the Christian faith and the old Roman spirit? Was not Luther's German Christianity a valuable and distinct contribution to Christianity? So then, pray be careful that you call your American or English Christianity a universal religion, and condemn my Japanese Christianity as national and sectional. . . I have seen no more sorrowful figures than Japanese who imitate their American or European missionary teachers by being converted to the faith of the latter.[86]

## Conclusion

For many Japanese, both Christian and non-Christian, Uchimura has become a paradigmatic figure because in his intense loyalty to transcendent reality he also intensely loved his country with great personal integrity and independence. He refused to compromise his principles when the events of national history by-passed him, but he also refused to withdraw from the life of his nation. His leadership inspired a movement of moral men and women who served their country with dedication and a critical conscience.[87] His personal formula for the moral or "true Japanese" was summed up five years before his death in his famous "Two J's" statement, composed in parallel English and Japanese:

I love two J's and no third; one is Jesus, and the other is Japan.
I do not know which I love more, Jesus or Japan.
I am hated by my countrymen for Jesus' sake as yaso,[88] and I am disliked by foreign missionaries for Japan's sake as national and narrow.

86. Zenshū, XV, p. 578 ff.
87. As Otis Cary pointed out in his 1956 article: "Correspondence," p. 459: "The past two Presidents of the University of Tokyo are well-known as Uchimura followers. They merely head the list which includes the present and only post-war Chief Justice of the Supreme Court, two distinguished Ministers of Education in post-war Cabinets, three Ambassadors in the foreign service three prominent scientists and many men prominent in the arts and professions as well as business."
88. A derogatory term for a Christian.

No matter; I may lose all my friends but I cannot lose Jesus and Japan.

For Jesus' sake, I cannot own any other God than His Father as my God and Father; and for Japan's sake, I cannot accept any faith which comes in the name of foreigners. Come salvation; come death; I cannot disown Jesus and Japan; I am emphatically a Japanese Christian, though I know missionaries do not like that name.

Jesus and Japan; my faith is not a circle with one centre: it is an ellipse with two centres. My heart and mind revolve around the two dear names. And I know that one strengthens the other; Jesus strengthens and purifies my love for Japan; and Japan clarifies and objectifies my love for Jesus. Were it not for the two, I would become a mere dreamer, a fanatic, an amorphous universal man.[89]

89. Zenshū, XV, p. 599 ff.

# NON-CHURCH CHRISTIANITY AND JAPAN'S CULTURAL IDENTITY

Carlo Caldarola

## I

This paper deals with a singular aspect of indigenization of Chrisitianity in the world and points to its relevance in the context of the recent developing trends in the field of sociology of religion. By indigenization we mean a process of cultural synthesis in which elements of a certain culture (donor culture) are accepted and integrated into another culture (recipient culture). Cultural borrowing is an old phenomenon in the history of humanity. In fact, the growth of human culture as a whole has been due to the ability of all societies to borrow elements from other cultures and to incorporate them into their own. This cultural exchange from one society to another is commonly known among social scientists as diffusion. With regard to the object of exchange, it is needless to say that there is a significant difference between material and spiritual culture in the process of borrowing and integration. Material culture or technology can be transplanted without substantial modifications. But spiritual culture which includes such social phenomena as religion, philosophy, and art is so strictly linked to inner thoughts, feelings, and the aspirations of the people that it is extremely difficult for it to be communicated and accepted without significant adaptation.[1]

The problem of communication and acceptance is critical in the case of religion, which is supposed to evoke a commitment to a faith and to shape and

This article, with minor editorial changes, is reprinted with permission from the International Journal of Contemporary Sociology, Vol. 10, No. 4, (October 1973), pp. 236-47. It is based on my research on the indigenization of Christianity in Japan which has now been published in full as Uchimura Kanzō to mukyōkai (Shinkyō shuppansha, 1978).

1. Ralph Linton, The Study of Man (Appleton-Century-Crofts, 1936), p. 339.

influence the entire personality of the believer. The problem becomes even more acute when foreign missionaries act not only as agents of ideology, that is as heralds of a new message, but also as institutionalizing agents who attempt to transplant the theology, liturgy, and ecclesiastical organization in exactly the same institutional forms that developed in their native culture. In the case of Christianity, the difficulty of exposure to missionaires, then is not so much conversion to Christ but conversion to new forms of cultural life. Generally speaking, missionary concern with indigenization has not gone beyond the establishment of a vernacular liturgy, an indigenous clergy, and an indigenous hierarchy rigidly patterned after the "orthodox" lines of the countries of origin. Obviously, those institutions are not the spontaneous expression of a spirituality which has been maturing through a long and genuine interaction between Christian ideas and local culture; they are forms built in cooperation with indigenous people but are entirely determined by and functionally dependent on the outside.

However, in the process of indigenization which follows the initial acceptance of new values, we have to consider also the reaction of the indigenous people. In this regard, we can distinguish three types of attitudes. One might be called an attitude of passive receptivity in which the subject accepts the teaching of the missionaries and tries to conform to their standards with great submission and docility. The result of this may be that the individual identifies himself with the new ideology to the point that he becomes alienated from his own culture, a stranger in his own country. A second type of attitude is compromise, by which the convert tries to interlace two cultural systems into a life pattern. In his eclecticism, he quite naturally wants all the advantages of each system and none of the disadvantages of either; he relies on one or another cultural aspect according to the needs of the moment. In practice, however, he definitely identifies with the tradition of his culture and tries to subject the new values to it. A third possibility is that of a selective indigenizer who carefully picks the essential aspects of both the cultures so as to produce a new culture out of the interaction of the old and new. This might be called a "grafting attitude" which attempts to graft a new Christian life onto those elements of the old tradition that appear as potential seeds of Christianity. In the following pages we will illustrate exactly the socio-cultural dynamics involved in the grafting process as it appears from a peculiar case of indigenization of Christianity in Japan.

After having been banned for 250 years, Christianity was reintroduced into Japan in the latter part of the nineteenth century under diplomatic pressure from the western powers. Some Japanese accepted it immediately, hoping to find in it a workable ideological motivation for the development of a renaissance out of the ruins of feudalism. In this context, Protestant Christianity had a particular appeal as the enlightened religion which had accelerated the modernization of western countries. Many ambitious young men, children of declassed samurai families, sought to gain influence in society by adopting Christianity, especially American Puritanism, which was seen as a form of higher morality able to integrate with the traditional Confucian ethics.

While eager to accept Christianity as a new code of ethics, however, Japanese Christians were not at all concerned with western ecclesiastical institutionalism--theology, liturgy, church organization--which seemed completely unrelated to their historico-cultural environment and therefore devoid of any emotional interest. But although they wanted to be strongly independent, in practice the Japanese Christians repeatedly failed to create an independent church organization and had to rely on foreign mission boards. The result was an undesired affiliation with the different western denominations. In reaction to this anomalous situation, a group of Japanese Christians finally decided to eliminate all church organization and to proclaim an indigenous churchless Christianity. This group originally developed out of the Sapporo Band, one of the three famous Bands formed by American missionaries in Japan in the second half of the last century, and was spearheaded by Uchimura Kanzō under the name of Mukyōkai or "non-church" Christianity.[2]

Mukyōkai makes a basic distinction between the "Ecclesia" and the "Church"; while accepting the former as a fellowship of believers in Christ, it rejects the Church as an institution. Consequently, the movement neither has any sacraments, liturgy, professional clergy, or church buildings, nor maintains national headquarters, membership rolls, or any kind of statistics. The essential framework of non-churchism is based on Bible study groups which aim at fostering faith in Christ and creating a fellowship of true believers.

2. Aside from my own recent study of the subject, only a few western theologians and missionaries have given some consideration to the mukyōkai movement. See, for example, W. H. H. Norman, "Non-Church Christianity in Japan," International Review of Missions, XLVI, No. 184 (1957), pp. 380-94; R.P. Jennings, Jesus, Japan, and Uchimura Kanzō (Kyōbunkan, 1958) and Emil Brunner, "A Unique Christian Mission: The Mukyōkai Movement in Japan," in Walter Leibrecht (ed.), Religion and Culture: Essays in Honor of Paul Tillich (Harper & Brothers, 1958), pp. 287-90. In Japanese see the following works by the Mukyōkai scholars: Sekine Masao, Mukyōkai Kirisutokyō (Non-Church Christianity), Atene Bunten, No. 44, Kōbundō, 1949; and Kurosaki Kokichi, Hitotsu no Kyōkai (One Church), Seimeisha, 1951.

The gathering place is usually a private home or rented hall. The meetings consist of hymn-singing, reading and explanation of the Bible, and a short spontaneous prayer appropriate to the times.

There is no formal training for Bible teachers. Anyone who feels inspired by God may form his own independent group and teach the Bible. Most of the teachers are regularly employed elsewhere, quite a few of them as university or high school teachers; some of them have studied Greek and Hebrew and produced scholarly Biblical works, which form an outstanding contribution to the indigenous Christian literature. A group automatically disintegrates when its leader dies or retires. In these cases each disciple can decide independently either to join another group, to start a new group of his own, or simply to retire from all group participation. Occasionally, small groups of disciples may decide to meet weekly, taking turns giving the lectures. In any case, the emergence of new groups does not involve any issues of "succession" from the old.

In their conception of Christian life, the Mukyōkai people are characterized by a strongly puritanic attitude. A deep sense of sin and justification by the Cross lies at the core of their spiritual experience, which is aimed at developing intimate and mystical relations with Christ. Thus, faith does not consist in a formal intellectual assent to prescribed dogmatic formulas, but in a thorough witnessing of the Gospel in daily life and in the experiencing of inner conflict and denial of this world. In the idealized puritan life, special emphasis is placed on the sense of loyalty to Christ, duty, detachment, sincerity, purity, and honesty. The puritan attitude is also strongly manifested socially by an uncompromising stand against what are considered to be the evil aspects of society. Forming a non-institutionalized group, non-church Christians are not concerned with assuring the survival of the group in times of turmoil; therefore they feel free to speak out against political and moral corruption, although they do so always as individuals. Ever since the Meiji Era, they have vigorously supported their spiritual and theistic perspectives in opposition to the invading current of materialism. Politically, they consistently opposed Shintō nationalism and Japanese imperialism, and paid a high price for such opposition.

The Mukyōkai concept has attracted people from all walks of life and from all social strata in Japan. It has appealed particularly to the Japanese intelligentsia: university professors, scholars, graduate students, and other professionals. All age groups are represented in the movement; however, young adults predominate, with 60 percent of the members falling in the age bracket 21-40 years. In contrast to the institutional Church in Japan, the majority (about 60 percent) of the believers are adult males. Despite the small number of believers (about 50,000), the influence of the movement among Japanese Christians is remarkable. It is estimated that approximately 25 percent of the Mukyōkai believers are drop-outs from Christian churches. The common reason for turning to the non-church movement appears to be a basic dissatisfaction with various aspects of the institutional churches, e.g., their emphasis on orthodoxy, liturgical formalism, ecclesiastical rules, financial budgets, the mediocrity of the clergy, and the tendency of the Church to compete or compromise with secular institutions. Besides, there are serious indications that a rather large number of Church Christians belong spiritually to the Mukyōkai movement, and consider it to be the genuine form of Japanese Christianity.

It is significant to notice that, in the mind of the Mukyōkai leaders, non-churchism is not to be considered as a sect denying the Church, and therefore establishing a kind of "non-church Church." The "non" of "non-church" does not only mean non-sacraments, non-liturgy, and non-theology, and other parameters; it is also a paradoxical "non" affirming a determinate reality, the reality of a true fellowship in Christ, through the denial of the Church institution. Thus, Mukyōkai should be defined in its truly protestant spirit as a perpetual protest against its own tendency to crystallize in specific forms, against the spirit of the world and against the institutionalism of the existing churches. Its reality is that of an organism in dynamic tension between its own life, the faith in Christ, and its major opponent, the spirit of the world of which churchism is a part. Only through a complete and continual denial of this opponent can Mukyōkai preserve its life in Christ and move constantly towards its goal of an invisible, spiritual Church.

For Mukyōkai Christians, churches badly need a second reformation which should bring Protestantism to its logical mission, by purifying from the Church all traces of institutionalism, and making it a free communion of souls. But in their opinion, this reformation cannot be accomplished by western people, who always tend to rationalize the spiritual in the vain attempt to preserve it from dissolution. The new reformation instead must be the task of Asians, for they, like the Hebrew prophets and apostles, are able to grasp the spirit as spirit, apart from definite forms. Moreover, the Japanese, since they are free of the Church tradition, are the most able to proclaim a churchless Christianity, to launch a new experiment in the spiritual history of mankind, to begin Christianity anew.[3] It is commonly believed,

3. See particularly, Uchimura Kanzō, Chosakushū (Selected Works), Iwanami

however, that to fulfill this mission Japan does not need to send out missionaries, or even issue special publications in foreign languages. Mukyōkai Christians feel that foreigners in general are still too arrogant to give due consideration to Japanese thoughts on Christianity. More important, Mukyōkai leaders resist any planned diffusion of their ideas lest the impression be generated that non-church Christianity is an organized movement. They feel that when the west is ripe for the non-church idea, foreign scholars will become interested and spread it to the western world.

## II

In an attempt to give a theoretical explanation of the above phenomenon, it is important to contrast the two basic value orientations that distinguish Japanese culture from western culture. It is a well known fact to the students of culture that the rational attitude of western people emphasizes the universal rather than the particular aspect of things, a tendency that appears markedly evident in the European philosophy with its stress upon abstract ideas and universal principles. The result is an universal ethic which lays down uniform rules or principles to be observed by every man at any place at any time. This obviously leads in religion towards a rationalization of the object of faith and the institutionalization of religion.

In opposition to this rational universalistic tendency stands the Japanese traditionalism with its emphasis on a particularistic ethic in which the individual is considered as linked to a specific particular group, such as family, community, nation. This attitude of stressing a limited specific human nexus tends to disregard any allegedly universal norm. This explains why the greatest virtue in traditional Japan was to sacrifice one's self for the interest of the feudal lord, the family, or the community. This also explains why the forms of expression of the Japanese language have always been more oriented to sensitive and emotional nuances than logical rigor, and why Japanese thinking has not been developed in an impersonal and logical direction and has been unable to produce strong philosophical and religious systems similar to those that emerged in China, India, or western countries.[4]

Shoten, 1953, VII, pp. 52, 218 ff.; Fujii Takeshi, Zenshū (Complete Works), Iwanani Shoten, 1931, III, pp. 473 ff.

4. See in this regard Hajime Nakamura, Ways of Thinking of Eastern Peoples: India-China-Tibet-Japan (East-West Center Press, 1964), pp. 345 ff.

Although the Japanese people came in contact with highly conceptualized forms of Buddhism and Confucianism, they rejected their metaphysical speculations and assimilated only what looked to be more convenient to their practical organization of life. Similarly, in the modern period, despite the profound innovations introduced by industrialization and bureaucratization, Japanese particularism seems to have emerged victorious from the confrontation; in their efforts to reconcile the East with the West, the Japanese have unconsciously managed to preserve their cultural identity and have succeeded in producing a new revised form of particularism.[5] In such a syncretism foreign elements are accepted only in those aspects and insofar as they prove to be useful for some specific purposes and may fit well with the indigenous tradition of the country.

Following these particularistic tendencies, the Japanese mind directs its interests more in the domain of immediate experience, grasping the object of knowledge with a sharp act of intuition. Consequently, in the field of religion the Japanese mind is more inclined towards a practical stand. Throughout the religious tradition of the country, the Japanese mind has never been inclined to distinguish between the subjective and the objective, between self-experience and other-experience, between feeling and rational knowledge. Religious truth is primarily the result of a diffuse unarticulated feeling (*kimochi*) which cannot be expressed in a series of dogmatic articles. This conception naturally leads to mysticism, that is to absorption, identification, or union with the divinity or an equivalent form of it. The Confucianist aspires to identify himself with Heaven, the Taoist-Zen with a state of non-differentiation, the Buddhist with Nothingness, the Shintoist with a particular deity. Religion to the Japanese is experience and feeling rather than exact dogmas of faith.

Zen Buddhism with its characteristic "apprehension" through direct grasping is a typical example of the non-reflective, and immediate power of experience. As Suzuki Daisetz states, "if the Greeks taught us how to reason and Christianity what to believe, it is Zen that teaches us to go beyond logic to find an absolute point where no dualism in whatever form obtains."[6] Zen never "explains, but indicates"; what Zen advocates is a direct appeal to the facts of personal experience, meaning "to get at the fact first-hand and not

5. See Robert N. Bellah, "Japan's Cultural Identity: Some Reflections on the work of Watsuji Tetsurō," *The Journal of Asian Studies*, XXIV, No. 4 (August 1965), pp. 573-94.
6. Daisetz Suzuki, *Zen Buddhism and Its Influence on Japanese Culture* (Kyoto: The Eastern Buddhist Society, 1938), p. 235.

through any intermediary whatever this may be."[7] Actually, the Zennist not only defies reason and logic, but he also takes pride in transcending the usual channels of thinking. With the intuitive power of Zen he reaches into the innermost recess of the human soul, an ultimate reality which transcends all individual differences and temporary mutations, the reality of the soul or mind as a participant in the cosmic reality.

In the Japanese religious contact with nature, the deities are to be found in mountains and woods, cherry blossoms and autumn leaves, rivers and gardens, wherever one may feel their presence; seldom are they found in large temples. Whatever gives peace of mind and harmonizes the center of personal life with the center of the universe is a religious experience. When a Japanese goes to visit a place where the deities dwell, he has a feeling that he is coming across something mysterious, he is having a sort of religious experience which cannot be measured by standards of truth but by mood alone. A typical example is the ordinary act of worship to a Shinto divinity. A faithful believer who comes to a Shinto shrine, stands still in front of it, bows deeply, closes his eyes, claps his hands, and tries to feel the deity deep in his heart. He does not attempt to build up any rational proof for the existence of an invisible deity, nor does he perhaps even know the individual name of the deity he worships. These things are not important for him. What really matters is whether or not he feels the existence of the deity directly in his heart. In his immediate perception of the god, the believer comes to an exchange of favors with him; the god dispenses blessings (on) and the believer gratefully makes return for those blessings (hōon). Thus, a sense of god-centered filial piety develops, which implies loyalty to the pre-established ideals cherished by the god. Salvation, in its broadest meaning, has been traditionally connected with the various forms of filial piety and loyalty. In short, Japanese religion is characterized by the feeling of participation or communion with the absolute. It cannot be exteriorized, nor is it based on intellectual assent; rather it is a diffuse sense of rightness and happiness.[8]

In accordance with this picture of Japan's cultural traits, it is no wonder that a natural and spontaneous indigenization of Christianity by the

7. Suzuki, Essays in Zen Buddhism (first series), (Luzac & Company, 1927), pp. 6-8.
8. For the above features of Japanese religiosity see particularly: Kishimoto Hideo, "Some Japanese Cultural Traits and Religions," in Charles A. Moore, ed., The Japanese Mind (East-West Center Press, 1967), pp. 110-21; and Joseph J. Spae, Japanese Religiosity (Oriens Institute for Religious Research, 1971).

Japanese had to follow the master lines of the spiritual tradition of the country. This explains why to Mukyōkai Christians it is so natural to consider faith not as an intellectual assent to a certain defined truth, but as a living experience, as a practice of loyalty to a specific person, the Person of Christ. This personal commitment to Christ for the Japanese does not need to be expressed in prescribed dogmatic moral or liturgical formulas.

With regard to the way of teaching ethics and religion, in Japan, the particularistic feature has been traditionally strong. The moral philosophies of Buddhism and Confucianism converged in their emphasis on the identity of the individual with his social milieu. The tendency to confine absolute values to a limited human group was characterized by a similarly absolute devotion to a specific individual as the concrete symbol of the group. The old saying, "a faithful servant does not acknowledge two masters," was most concretely realized in the religious sector. Unlike traditional western thinkers, who based their ideas on the universal law of reason, Japanese intellectuals drew upon the authority of the teacher himself. As a result of this emphasis upon a concrete individual as symbol of a religion or group, faith becomes essentially a belief in that person as a real person, a founder or teacher, and as an ideal person, a specific Buddha or Bodhisattva. The personae become so intermingled in the resulting faith that it is difficult to differentiate them; the important characteristic is the focus of a specific person. Thus, whereas the Indians and Chinese worship Buddha as an embodiment of truth and eternal law, the Japanese tend to venerate him as a person who achieved all the ideal virtues through ascetic practices.[9]

The absolute value placed on a limited and specific type of human relationship centered on a hierarchical authority also gave rise to a number of segmented religious sects, each characterized by a specific inheritance from a master and therefore incompatible with the others. The difference between Indo-Chinese and Japanese Buddhism is quite marked in this respect. Whereas Buddhist sects in India and China are schools characterized primarily by differences of doctrine, sects in Japan are usually centered upon the person of their founder, who is venerated both in himself and in his successors. This sense of absolute devotion to a specific individual enables us to understand the great influence wielded by religious leaders in Japan, and the charisma exerted by the personality of the founder of the so-called new religions in the modern period is but a continuity of Japanese tradition in this respect.

9. See Nakamura, op. cit., pp. 459-60.

Another aspect of Japanese particularism relevant to our concerns is its manifestation in education following the Confucian tradition. The social reorganization occurring during the early seventeenth century encouraged the formation of private academies where independent Confucian scholars (jusha) gathered their disciples to study disciplines of common interest.[10] Within these academies, education was seen as a matter of personal contact between teacher and pupil. Young men who intended to be professional scholars in some branch of knowledge might even board at the house of the teacher, just as in the case of an apprentice learning a skill from a master craftsman. Even after the development of the fief school system during the Tokugawa period, schools remained centered around some distinguished teacher who could attract students from many different areas because of his personal qualities. The relationship between student and teacher remained one of discipleship rather than institutional interplay; the student was understood to be a pupil of a particular teacher, rather than just at the school, even though he might change teachers as he progressed in learning.

The teacher-disciple relation was a close one in which the teacher played the role of guide and benevolent protector. The personality and teachings of his mentor exerted great power over the development of the student. The word sensei thus referred to "a venerable or beloved teacher or master." Respect and filial piety toward the master were inculcated as an absolute value: "keep seven feet behind your teacher and never tread on his shadow" was a popular saying of the Japanese Confucian tradition. As a result of the awe and respect with which a teacher was regarded, knowledge was received by the students as a gift to be accepted with humility, not to be discussed or improved upon and never to be questioned. Japanese teachers of this traditional type would take no fees for their work, for it was considered to be a spiritual mission which could not be exchanged for material goods.

The teachers generally followed the philosophy of Chu Hsi (1130-1200) and Wang Yang-ming (1472-1529), emphasizing knowledge as wisdom without making any distinction between intellectual and moral training. Thus, an individual became a teacher himself not on the basis of a certain intellectual achievement, but because he had come to possess a complex of spiritual and moral virtues enabling him to become a living example to his pupils. The role of a Confucian scholar was to be a moral philosopher. Convinced that the

10. See in this regard, John W. Hall, "The Confucian Teacher in Tokugawa Japan," in David S. Nivision and Arthur F. Wright, eds., Confucianism in Action (Stanford University Press, 1959), pp. 268-301; and Ronald P. Dore, Education in Tokugawa Japan (University of California Press, 1965).

books of the Sages revealed the ultimate truth, the scholar provided a sound moral and philosophical training for the acceptance of a naturally ordained social hierarchy and for the practice of an appropriate morality by responsible members of society.

With regard to ecclesiastical organization, the Japanese never had in their tradition any institution comparable to the Church in the west. Although Buddhism has a highly organized and complex institutional structure of temples and priests, it never achieved the status of a religion in the western sense; during the Tokugawa period, everyone was supposed to be affiliated with a Buddhist temple, but this was, in reality, a form of political control and census registry, devoid of any religious significance. On the other hand, Confucianism, which never achieved any institutional form, provided to the entire country principles for meaningful moral and social behavior.

Recalling these features of the tradition, Uchimura commented: "Priests we have, but they are essentially temple-keepers and not teachers of Truth and Eternal Verities. All our moral reformers were teachers, 'pedagogues' who taught the things of the spirit while they taught letters and science."[11] Since the informal school tended also to fulfill the function of the Church, the Japanese developed their entire social, moral, and religious personality within the student-teacher relationship. This may explain why the Bible-study groups structure of Mukyōkai fits with the traditional teacher-disciple (sensei-deshi) relationship. In this sense the movement may be seen as a modern development of the traditional private schools (juku) where independent Confucian scholars used to gather bands of disciples to study a discipline of common interest. This type of structure, in the Japanese cultural tradition, is the most simple and flexible, and allows to be perpetuating of faith through meetings of individuals, without, however, the risk of crystallizing itself in institutional forms.

## III

The foregoing considerations have shown how the churchless type of Christianity is truly congenial with the traditional particularistic pattern of Japanese social relations. As religion for the Japanese is an intimate spontaneous experience of the individual soul, it obviously cannot be enclosed in rigid institutional forms. Though a teacher may be needed and a complete

11. Uchimura Kanzō, Zenshū, XV, p. 842.

submission to his guidance may be required as in the case of Zen in order to help remove what hinders the experience of the supernatural, nevertheless this experience itself is strictly personal and incommunicable and it is not bound to any other man nor to any specific institution on earth. Moreover, in the case of non-churchism it seems that Christianity has emphasized even more the traditional freedom of the individual in his religious experience, trying to reduce to a minimum the role of the teacher himself. This original context of spiritual freedom and particularistically oriented structure sum up the Japaneseness of Mukyōkai and suggest to the puzzled western mind the possibility of perpetuating a movement without the necessity of institutionalized structures.

By the same token, the above considerations explain also why western Christian churches do not appeal to the Japanese. Obviously, the fact that Christianity is a foreign import is no reason for its rejection; so is Buddhism and so are the sciences and techniques which have modernized Japan. But, in the case of the Christian churches, "foreignness" is equated with the "arrogant exclusiveness" of westerners. Whereas Buddhism entered Japan and enriched its spiritual life, Christianity, instead, did not seek to enrich or fulfill but to displace, and offers a western Christianity with its institutions, theology, social and political ideas, and behavior patterns, which the Church generally identifies with the Gospel. The objection is essentially levelled against Christian missions which are seen as an expression of western religious imperialism threatening to change Japan's cultural identity in favor of a western Church, western thought, western symbolism, western organization and way of life. In the context it is easy to explain the psychological reaction of those Japanese Christians who, in the face of danger of losing their cultural identity, stand to reassess their spiritual tradition and to proclaim their messianic function in the world through the affirmation of non-churchism.

This affirmation of a non-church Christianity naturally poses a challenge to western sociologists who would study a non-institutional type of Christianity. As is known, the literature of sociology of religion is packed with studies on the institutional aspects of religious life. Accordingly, sociologists have often used scales and indexes to measure how people relate to the institution of the Church. These measures are often conceived in unilateral terms and implicitly assume that the greater the number of dogmas a person believes or the higher his frequency of Church attendance and the larger his donations to the Church, the stronger and more genuine is his faith. Such an approach while useful for certain purposes is, however, obviously inadequate when one has to assess the salience and the function of religious beliefs for the individual, and it would be meaningless and inappropriate for the study of non-institutional religions and particularly Mukyōkai. The Japanese instance clearly stresses the necessity of distinguishing between a "simply religious personality" and a "denominational religious personality," thereby urging us to apply new methods to study religiosity (as a personal committment to certain absolute values),[12] a point of pivotal significance today due to the increasing need for a separation of religion from its institutional parameters which is so strongly felt even in western countries.[13]

12. See Charles Y. Glock and Rodney Stark, Religion and Society in Tension, (Rand MacNally & Co., 1965), pp. 18-38.
13. Suffice it to mention here as examples of this trend the increasing spread of phenomena such as the underground church and the Catholic Pentecostals. See M. Boyd, The Underground Church (Sheed & Ward, 1968) and K. and D. Ranaghan, Catholic Pentecostals (Paulist Press Deus Books, 1969).

# THE THOUGHT OF UCHIMURA KANZŌ AND ITS RELEVANCE TO CONTEMPORARY AMERICAN RELIGION

Ohara Shin

A Japanese observer of American religious life in the late 1970s--especially a student of Uchimura Kanzō's teachings--is often confused by the evidence of conflicting trends. On the one hand, it appears that few Americans today attend church. Many seem to have become suspicious of traditional religious practices of mainline denominations, to have lost their zeal for institutionalized religion. There appears to be a widespread apathy toward religious institutions and practices. Church pews stand empty or are occupied only by senior citizens. Many Americans seem to have lost their identity as Christians. On the other hand, there is evidence that they are earnestly seeking something new and attractive in their inner world, seeking a spiritual comfort despite their apparent apathy. They have become tolerant of religious differences. Few seem to care any longer about the fine distinctions of Protestant denominations. Taken together, these tendencies suggest to me that many Americans have become what I call "churchless." by this I do not mean that they have no church to attend, for there are many empty church buildings which, in fact, are often used for cultural events! But they have no church in which they can make serious personal commitments. Despite the search for new types of religious expression among Asian religions and conservative or fundamentalist denominations, these Americans are left unsatisfied.

My point is that although Americans have become irreligious in an orthodox sense, they are still a fundamentally religious people. Their spiritual quest has not been satisfied by conventional religious leaders and teachings. Nor have they found satisfaction by turning east to non-Christian religions. What they may need, it seems to me, is a new definition of their own religion. It is in this context that I see the relevance of the thought of

This is a revised and expanded version of a paper delivered at the Uchimura Seminar held at Amherst College, Massachusetts, on March 31, 1977.

Uchimura Kanzō, especially his idea of "Mukyōkai" or "non-church" Christianity. Uchimura's thought provides the possibility of maintaining Christian faith in a relatively non-institutional and non-sacramental style, and yet of preserving the essence of the Christian spirit in contemporary secular and pluralistic society. While his thought may have some strong Japanese implications, his idea of preserving the firm individual piety of Christian faith by following the idea of non-church Christianity has within it strong universalistic elements.

To write about Uchimura is a very complicated and difficult task. He lived in a time when nearly all Japanese were turning West. Fukuzawa Yukichi, one of Japan's spiritual leaders in the Meiji era, emphasized the importance of "escaping from the East, and entering into the West." Uchimura himself, following his education at Amherst, emphasized the necessity "turning to the East," not to escape from the west or from Christianity, but rather to strengthen his own faith in Christ. Uchimura also emphasized the importance of maintaining Christian faith without the use of any institutional or sacramental means. In this way Uchimura tried to find in the east a way of preserving the essence of the Christian faith of the west. His was an effort to adjust Christianity according to the cultural climate, and yet it was also an effort to fight for the conventional ways of maintaining Christian faith.

It is ironic that Uchimura and his friends in Sapporo, usually called the "Sapporo Band," were in the 1870s and 1880s among the most Americanized people in Japan. Most of their schooling was in English, and their correspondence, except with their parents, was all written in English. Yet it was from this group that a man like Uchimura could emerge to call for a Christian faith adapted to Japan without any formal institutions.

The idea of a non-institutional faith and a Japanese version of the Christian faith were the two things Uchimura wanted to bequeath to future generations--not buildings, institutions, or appointed disciples. But he seems in fact to have left many things to his countrymen. The Mukyōkai movement is an example of adaptation by the young son of an ex-samurai as he faced the new western thought in the early days of modern Japan. Uchimura tried to reconcile the east and the west, that is, to reconcile "Japan" with "Jesus." The late nineteenth century New England theology was, for Uchimura, evangelistic faith rather than the new tides of Unitarianism. That is why he chose to study at Amherst instead of Harvard.

My point is that Uchimura tried to adapt orthodox Christianity, which was in those days known only as western religion, into a more indigenous form for the Japanese, so that they might be able to accept it more naturally and amicably. His effort deserves our attention in a wider context; and what follows is an attempt to examine the relevance of his ideas in today's chaotic religious situation.[1] The discussion delineates four themes: the seemingly provocative and irritating character of the "Mukyokai" movement; the paradoxical and dialectical aspects of their group formation; contrasts between the institutional and non-institutional approach to Christianity in Japan; and the recent tendency to "turn East" among Americans and its relationship with Uchimura as the founder of "Mukyōkai" Christianity.[2]

### Characteristics of the "Mukyōkai" Movement

"Mukyōkai" is the word used to designate Uchimura's religious position of rejecting the organized church. It is usually rendered in English as "non-church" but a more accurate translation would be "churchless," that is, Christianity without a church. The term "non-church" or "no-church" does not convey the idea accurately. "Mukyōkai" suggests radical implications to many traditionally orthodox Christians in Japan. Perhaps it was through Emil Brunner's paper in the Festschrift for Paul Tillich in the 1950s that the term "Mukyōkai" became widely known in the west.[3] In 1956 Time magazine published a special issue on the Mukyōkai people in Japan and introduced to the American public the work and thought of Uchimura and his followers.[4] Because of its seemingly radical and provocative elements, many people have been puzzled by the word "non-church." The term itself surely invites misunderstanding among conventional Christians who are uninformed about the nature of Japanese culture or about the actual activities of Mukyōkai people.

The life and work of Uchimura Kanzō are considered to be the single most original contribution as yet made by a Japanese to the world of

1. The following is based on my book, Hyōden Uchimura Kanzō, (Uchimura Kanzō: His Life and Thought), Chūō kōronsha, 1976, 400 pp.
2. I wish to explore here the churchless situation of the American people not from a negative or critical standpoint, but rather in a constructive vein, following Uchimura's idea of "Mukyōkai."
3. Emil Brunner, "A Unique Christian Mission: The Mukyokai ('Non-Church') Movement in Japan," in Walter Leibrecht (ed.), Religion and Culture: Essays in Honor of Paul Tillich, New York: Harper & Brothers, 1959, pp. 287-290.
4. Time, April 23, 1956.

Christianity. He was first drawn seriously to Christianity under the pressure of older students at Sapporo Agricultural College from which he was graduated in 1881. William S. Clark, the president of Massachusetts Agricultural College and an ardent Christian, had spent eight months in Sapporo in 1876-77 helping establish the new school. He had accepted the job of teaching ethics on condition that he could also teach the Bible, and the Governor of Hokkaido had reluctantly, but officially, granted permission. From this single act emerged the band of Christian students to which Uchimura belonged. Although Clark had left Sapporo before Uchimura's arrival, his teachings were transmitted to young Uchimura by the older students who had become Christians before Uchimura reached Sapporo.

Uchimura and his friends signed the "Covenant of Believers in Jesus" which Clark had written for them before his return home in 1877. The students formed a small informal church in which they became baptized members. They continued their services and fellowship in this way after graduation; and with the sympathetic understanding of a Methodist missionary, M. C. Harris, laid plans to erect their own church building, which was to be known as the Sapporo Independent Church (Sapporo Dokuritsu Kyōkai). However, when Harris was replaced by Reverend Davidson the young men lost a sympathetic supporter for their independent church. Meanwhile, when two Episcopalian missionaries arrived in Sapporo, keen competition developed between them and the Methodist Davidson for the loyalty of the small congregation of the Sapporo Independent Church. Desiring to hold the young men in the Methodist fold, Davidson gave them $400 to purchase a building not realizing that they planned to use the building to gain more autonomy and become independent of the Methodist Church. When several Episcopal converts joined the church, even the Episcopal missionaries gave their support to the development of an Independent Church. Davidson strongly opposed separation, and requested that the money be returned. Surprised and incensed, Uchimura and his friends repaid the amount within a year at great personal sacrifice.

The evils and foolishness of "denominational rivalry" became plain in the minds of the young men, as did the necessity of financial independence from western missionaries. So Uchimura wrote in his spiritual autobiography written in English[5] "Sapporo Church is Independent. Joys inexpressible and

5. <u>How I Became a Christian</u>. This book was first published in Japan by Keiseisha on May 10, 1895, and later in the same year as <u>The Diary of a Japanese Convert</u> (F. H. Revell, 1895). It is included in <u>Uchimura Kanzō zenshū</u>, XV. (Hereafter <u>Zenshū</u> refers to the Iwanami edition of 1931-33.)

indescribable!" The Church continued to be self-supporting and grew rapidly. Uchimura wrote: "Independence is the conscious realization of one's own capabilities."[6]

After graduating as valedictorian of his class in 1881, Uchimura entered the Japanese Ministry of Agriculture and Commerce and served as a specialist in the marine products division. After three years of work there and the failure of his first marriage, he decided to go to America. As a youth, he had envisioned the United States as a "Christian country, a noble, puritan land of faith."[7] But the evil he saw in America saddened him, as Professor Hirakawa has pointed out in his essay.

At Amherst in 1885-87 Uchimura studied hard, liked his professors, reached a new understanding of the Gospel, and became a vibrant and ardent Christian. He was fully confirmed in the Gospel and became a vibrant and ardent Christian. Both at Sapporo and at Amherst, Uchimura encountered the Congregational New England faith. At the urging of President Julius H. Seelye of Amherst, Uchimura on graduation entered Hartford Theological Seminary in Connecticut in the fall of 1887, only to withdraw four months later with a feeling of frsutration and vague complaints of insomnia. His main disappointment in professional theology seems to have been that it was not appropriate to the Japanese climate. The seminary students were so secular and their casual references to a "twenty-dollar sermon" and "one thousand dollars with parsonage," made Uchimura suspicious about the professional ministry. They reminded him of men of religion in Japanese society, including the Christian ministers, who were in reality nothing but "economic parasites."

Back in Japan in 1889 Uchimura started on his career as a teacher, but could not manage to keep any job for long. Within eight years he taught in five different schools. He declined his friend Niishima's invitation to teach at Dōshisha because it was foreign supported. In January 1891 he provoked an intense controversy when he conscientiously refused to conform to the practice of bowing before the 1890 Imperial Rescript on Education. In the resulting uproar, he lost his job and became the target of attack by the leading philosopher of the time, Inoue Tetsujirō of Tokyo Imperial University, who contended that Christians were opposed to the Japanese national polity (kokutai) and that the "traitor" Uchimura was an outstanding example of this.[8]

6. Zenshū, XV, ch. 4.
7. Ibid., XV, ch. 6.
8. For further details, see Ohara, Hyōden Uchimura Kanzō, pp. 93-148.

Failing as a teacher, Uchimura turned to journalism as a social critic and reformer, contributing articles and essays to leading magazines and newspapers in both English and Japanese. During his lifetime he was involved in a succession of short-lived jobs as a writer. The publishing of personal monthly magazines played a significant role in keeping regular contact with his increasing readers and followers throughout Japan.[9] Ironically, it was partly because of his lese majesty incident that Uchimura was famous enough to sell books widely among the Japanese. But the same incident brought him into conflict with the Government over his pacifism and social criticism. In his early writings Uchimura wrote many essays and articles on the Sino-Japanese War (1894-95), the Russo-Japanese War (1904-05), the Ashio Copper Mine Pollution Case (1890s), and other significant social and political events. But later he devoted most of his energy to writing and teaching on his own. It was in these pursuits that he felt his mission, and he gathered around him a group of able young men. The shift from indirect efforts of social reform through secular publications to direct Christian journalism deepened his philosophical and theological sense.[10]

Uchimura founded no institutional Church nor formulated any systematic theology of his own. He simply propagated forcefully a new form of Christian faith reflecting his fierce spirit of "independence" of mind and faith: Uchimura called his idea of Christian faith "Mukyōkai," "Churchless Christianity," or "Japanese Christianity." About Mukyōkai he wrote:

> Mukyokai does not have the negative meaning one sees in anarchism or nihilism; it does not attempt to overthrow anything. "Non-Church" is the Church for those who have no

9. In February of 1897 Uchimura joined the staff of the <u>Yorozu chōhō</u> as its chief English writer. In May of the following year he resigned and started his own magazine called <u>Tokyo dokuritsu zasshi</u> (Tokyo Independent Magazine). In 1900 it was discontinued after two years, and he again joined the <u>Yorozu chōhō</u> as a guest writer, while at the same time beginning his new monthly magazine named <u>Seisho no kenkyū</u> (The Biblical Studies) which was his most successful undertaking and which lasted through 357 issues. In 1901 he began another magazine, <u>The Mukyōkai</u> (Non-Church), which lasted only 18 months. Some years later Uchimura also edited and published for two years an English language magazine, <u>The Japan Christian Intelligencer</u>, which lasted from March 1926 to February 1928.

10. My position differs from that of Ienaga Saburō and Arima Tatsuo. Cf. Ienaga, <u>Kindai seishin to sono genkai</u> (The Modern Spirit and Its Limits), Kadokawa shoten, 1950, pp. 55-170; and Arima, <u>The Failure of Freedom: A Portrait of Modern Japanese Intellectuals</u> (Harvard University Press, 1969), pp. 15-50.

> church. It is the dormitory for those who have no home, the orphanage or foundling home for the spirit. The negative character in the word Mukyokai should read "nai"—without—rather than "mu ni suru"—destroy—or "mushi suru"—despise. Are not those without money, without parents, without houses to be pitied? We believe there to be many sheep without shepherds, many Christians without churches. . .The true form of the Church is Mukyokai. There is no organized church in heaven. . . In heaven, there is neither baptism nor communion; neither teachers nor students: Mukyokai hopes to introduce this sort of Church to the world.[11]

Uchimura often overstated his case to get his point across. His negative emphasis was usually a literary device used to accentuate the positive. He used simple, single-thrust arguments to drive home his point, and it would be difficult to cull a doctrinal treatise on organized religion from his works. In most cases he was addressing specific concrete problems.

> The odium of Christianity is in its churches. Many have left and are leaving Christianity because they hate churches. But the priest and the surplice are not the one and same thing. The priest remains after you strip him of his surplice. You may hate the surplice and yet love the priest. Christianity minus churches is the Way, the Truth, and the Life. There is no reason for leaving Christ and His Gospel, because churches which are its institutional vestments are soiled and odious. Churchless Christianity will be the Christianity of the future. The seer of Patmos said: I saw no temple there.--Rev. 21:22.[12]

In short, Uchimura embraced Christianity "pure and simple"; "garnished and dogmatized" Christianity he rejected. He was content with the "undefinability of Christianity," which he did not think evidence of its nonexistence, much less of its fraudulence. Much that is thought to be Christianity, he felt, was in reality only its superstructure: "In reality we know more of what it is not than what it is." Thus he often repeated the simple assertion that "Christianity is Christ, not the Church."[13]

11. Zenshu, IX, pp. 210-13.
12. Zenshu, XV, p. 544.
13. Ibid., XV, pp. 149-150, 152-53. Zenshu, XV, contains many pages on Uchimura's view of "Church" and his idea of Mukyōkai.

By the term "Mukyōkai" Uchimura implied a non-institutional and non-sacramental Christian faith. He was, nonetheless, often seriously involved with the weddings and funerals of his friends and followers.[14] He also emphasized the Japanized form of Christianity in the context of cultural relativism, believing that the history of Japan was just as God-inspired as that of Israel. "God has never forsaken Japan: He never hath left himself without witness among Japanese. . ." "An idea that non-Christian Japan is less God's than Christian England or America is entirely false. . . And when I speak of God. . . I do not mean the Ruler of the Universe and Mankind. I mean the God of Luther and Calvin, of Dante and Milton, the Father of our Lord Jesus Christ."[15]

> Japanese Christianity is not a Christianity peculiar to the Japanese. It is Christianity received by Japanese directly from God without any foreign intermediary; no more, no less. In this sense, there is German Christianity, English Christianity. . . American Christianity. . . and in this sense, there will be, and already is, Japanese Christianity.[16]

While humbly and sometimes even conservatively trying to preserve the orthodox aspect of Christianity which was lost by the institutional and sacramental churches, believers of Mukyōkai emphasize the Kingdom of God above confirmation in particular churches. Uchimura held that it was a fundamental mistake to believe churches were indispensable for the salvation of individual souls. Their dislike of churches often gave others the impression that Mukyōkai Christians were antagonistic, hostile or negative towards the Church, and thus detrimental to Christianity. However, because of many earnest and sincere people in the Mukyōkai movement, most Japanese Christians today, whether they are church-goers or not, seem to acknowledge sympathetically the intention of Mukyōkai.

Instead of institutional church, the Bible is the authority for Mukyōkai people. All other authorities are to be subordinate to it. Uchimura especially urged the necessity for a deeper acquaintance with the Bible, and with this in mind formed a private Bible study group and published a monthly magazine named Seisho no Kenkyū (The Biblical Studies), the tone of which was practical and devout, rather than theologically dogmatic. He drew on modern

14. One of his disciples, Tsukamoto Toraji, emphasized "marriage" as a Sacrament for Mukyōkai Christians.
15. The Japan Christian Intelligencer, II, n. 1, pp. 3-4.
16. Zenshu, XV, p. 452.

thought and Biblical study, and hence his approach was never that of the fundamentalist but of rational modern man with the orthodox spirit of Christianity.

Among Mukyōkai people, no one ordains or is ordained. Each is a layman. He has no church or institution to fall back upon. But usually he happens to know a certain sensei[17] (teacher, master, or leader)whose Bible Study meeting he attends and where he is taught the Bible for several years. This has nothing to do with more than just getting together. Members are free in the matter of faith and usually they have no mutual organization or federation. One meeting may go this way and another meeting that way; there is no common form of worship or regular style of confession. But they do believe that "where there is a believer, there is a Church." When one becomes convinced that he himself should teach the Bible, he invites his own friends, neighbors or colleagues to his house or elsewhere to study the Bible with them.

Thus Mukyōkai Christians have a number of small cells here and there throughout Japan. A member of a meeting who happens to move to another city or town will usually begin studying the Bible there in like manner. Members subscribe to the many monthly magazines published privately by their sensei. In this case one's own sensei is often the owner and publisher of a small magazine through which one can keep in contact with the Bible and the sensei. The Bible Study meetings and small magazines are thus so spread throughout the country that making a precise count of them would be difficult. Since the printed word is just as important as the spoken word to the Mukyōkai Christian, there are a large number of periodicals by sensei with more than four to five thousand subscribers. A number of these lay leaders have also published Bible commentaries, Greek synopses and even concordances, which are often used by Japanese Biblical scholars because of their high academic quality. In so doing, they try to avoid dealing with subtle theological questions. Instead their intention is to concentrate on the Bible as it is rather than on man's thoughts about it. The literature produced by the spiritual leaders of Mukyōkai Christians often fill book shelves in Christian book stores in Japan.

17. The Japanese term "sensei" is usually translated as teacher, master, leader; sometimes it can imply a kind of boss, as well. "Sensei" can often be an equivalent of the role of minister or clergy in Christian countries, whereas Buddhist monks, Shintō priests, or Christian ministers often have less authority over the spiritual life of ordinary people than do "sensei."

Mukyōkai Christians are noted for their piety. They tend to speak in devotional terms, and their method of Bible study tends to be orthodox and academic. Mukyōkai Christians have attracted public attention through their earnest Bible study and pacifism. Some of them are known by their secular profession as university professors or intellectuals. Critics may complain about the highly intellectual character of their Bible study, for many Mukyōkai Christians strive to read the Bible either in Greek or in Hebrew, not to mention their knowledge of English or German. Many followers of Uchimura became either university professors or teachers; some are noted Biblical scholars, and others are famous for their intellectual influence or leadership. In this sense they are often highly respected among the Japanese people. Being Christians in Japan certainly makes them a minority, but this does not necessarily mean that they are a frustrated, unhappy lot.

Numerically a minority and yet very influential, pious, intellectual, and individually responsible—these are the characteristics which led to an appreciation of Mukyōkai Christians by adherents of pacifism during World War II. In fact Mukyōkai Christians have shown their greatest strength in pacifist social activities. However, their pacifism is different from that of Quakers. Mukyōkai Christians opposed the trend toward the Second World War, but once the war began, they gave their support out of a sense of national effort rather than yielding blindly to militarism. That is, while many Japanese Christians had to compromise with militarism during the war, many Mukyōkai people, individually, could oppose the attitude of Japanese militarism. In fact, they were able to utilize the strength of Mukyōkai in that they had no institution that could be attacked, whereas many church Christians had to compromise because of their vulnerable institutions.

## Mukyōkai Group Formation

Uchimura did not create a formal group of his young followers, but instead gathered them in an informal group.[18] This group remained for the most part non-institutional. Uchimura was extremely reluctant even to construct buildings for institutional purposes; and his Sunday Bible Study Meeting, which gathered in rented space, was dissolved upon his death. He

18. Uchimura and his followers to this day have met on Sundays without having any formal organization. His followers are able to keep such close fellowship and communication that their relationships last for their entire lives.

avoided forming fixed ties for these meetings. The participants had little chance to know each other: they met voluntarily only on Sundays, and members were not required to be baptized or registered as most Christians were. Uchimura charged an admission fee for his Sunday lectures rather than depending upon offerings by particpants as established churches did.[19]

Uchimura hated everything overly religious, and strictly avoided whatever seemed to imply formal rituals or professional religiosity. This was partly because he knew of many corrupt Buddhist priests in Japan and partly because of his experiences with different Christian denominations and ministers. In his meetings there was no holy communion or baptism as a condition for or as a sign of salvation.[20]

Group formation, therefore, did not create any formal ties to bind those seeking knowledge of the Christian faith. However, participants in a Mukyōkai group were not necessarily as separated from one another as this account might imply, for they did attend Sunday lectures and usually subscribed to at least one sensei's magazine. Uchimura and his close followers who became sensei in the Sunday lectures usually published their own small monthly magazines, which were sent directly to each participant's home. Mukyōkai can therefore be called a "paper-Church" in the sense that the magazines keep alive the relationship between a sensei and followers. The members dislike sacraments, but they value the magazines and books and are eager to receive their teachers' periodic publications.[21]

An analogy with the sensei (or shishō) of tea-ceremony, flower arrangement and so forth seems appropriate. In these relationships, the bonds are usually informal and personal. Members are most often personally related in small groups to the sensei and often meet at his or her home to undergo training or pursue the activity. The group relationship seems to be

19. This method, unique in the history of Japanese Christianity, has been continued by his followers, and seems by now to have become well established.
20. Occasionally, however, Uchimura baptized some persons if they eagerly asked him to do so as a sign of their confirmation of faith (although he himself was not an ordained minister of any denomination.) As for marriages and funerals, Uchimura was rather attentive to maintain his original style and tried to avoid the routine, conventional forms of conducting rituals. He and his followers conducted these services with their friends and relatives whenever they could, without asking professional clergy to preside. In this sense we may as well say that Mukyōkai Christians treated the rituals of funerals and marriages as if they were sacraments.
21. Mukyōkai Christians' unusual reliance on the written word seems to have opened them to the charge of being "too intellectual."

strengthened in this way and usually lasts for a long period—often the entire life of the participants. In Japan this kind of informal relationship has great vitality; it is often assumed to be a better and more intimate tie than a legal or official one.[22] This is an interesting paradox. The looser the organizational tie, the more amicable and intimate the personal involvement. This may reflect the spirit found in Japanese personal "contract" or commitment, for people seem to be bound in this type of relationship more amicably and intimately than in others.

Group members seldom enter into a formal contract; yet the absence of a contract does not weaken the relationship. On the contrary, it is a sign of personal trust. So, paradoxically, the looseness of the relationship has the effect of strengthening and deepening it. This kind of personal relationship is found even among white-collar workers or "salary men," for they, too, try to recreate a family-like kinship system among their peers in the midst of their highly industrialized society. Only when they can feel such an intimate relationship with others without any feeling of alienation, can they be free from the sense of being outsiders. This does not mean that Japanese neglect entirely formal contracts or bonds, but only that they often place informal ties above official or legal bonds.

Thus we can point out two characteristics of Mukyōkai group formation: first, a highly personal relationship to a group leader (sensei or shishō) who often reflects personal charisma (in Weber's sense); and second, an almost innate preference for loose relationships in their group formation. The link between sensei and seito—teacher/master and disciple/participants--can be found in an analogy with Zen Buddhism or in the case of a Confucian teacher/master who has some religious authority over his followers. Each sensei functions as a minor "shaman" who has charisma. He is not only the teacher for the religious subject concerned, but also an adviser in the personal affairs of his disciples—as in arranging marriages and choosing occupations.

In Mukyōkai groups, too, people come and meet each other for Sunday Bible study meetings; but they usually know little about each other. In actuality the closest human relationship in the meeting is often between the sensei

22. Many Japanese seem to pay less respect to legal or official matters than do westerners. This is also true when they face something "public" compared with something "private." Their different attitude toward the public and the private is a common characteristic of the Japanese. See Ohara Shin, "Gendai nihonjin no shakai ishiki" (Social Consciousness of the Contemporary Japanese), Hito to kokudo, May 1976.

and participants rather than a mutual relationship among participants. Here all we can find is an unofficial, loose bond in the form of personal attachments of each participant to the sensei. In the meeting the human relationship is "vertical" rather than horizontal; and this vertical relationship is often seen as analogous to the direct relationship with God. Yet this type of loose vertical organization seems, for the reasons described, to be stronger and last longer than the usual formal, impersonal bond in Japan.[23]

While personally committed to the sensei, Uchimura's followers developed only an informal personal contract rather than a regular Church-style organization. At Sapporo Agricultural College, Uchimura and his friends had wanted their church members to be independent of any denomination. Later in his Bible Study group, too, he tried to conduct his own independent meeting every Sunday without reference to any established church or denomination. When Uchimura and his friends at Sapporo signed the "Pledge," they assumed that their signatures were almost as valid as official baptism, even though they later submitted to baptism by an American missionary. Their preference for informality may have been due in part to the influence of their teacher at Sapporo, William S. Clark, who as a layman did not emphasize the centrality of the sacraments to his students.

Mukyōkai Christians also express their informal approach by deleting the word "nulla" from the phrase "Extra ecclesiae nulla salus" (outside of Church there is no salvation.)[24] However, their emphasis on a simple orthodox faith based on loose ties is sustained by their strong personal involvement with the sensei, God, and meetings for Bible study.

All of this is entirely entrusted to each individual's free choice as if it were an existential Christian movement. In fact, the Mukyōkai movement demands of its members something like an existential involvement instead of an acceptance of the sacraments and church institutions. This loose mode of group formation is, as we have seen, by no means peculiar to Mukyōkai people, for even today in Japan we can find numerous similar cases.[25] For instance,

23. One is reminded of the famous chapter by Maruyama Masao on the idea of takotsubo culture (octopus-pot culture). See Maruyama, Nihon no shisō (The Thought of the Japanese), Iwanami, 1961, p. 64.
24. This phrase was often used by one of Uchimura's disciples, Tsukamoto Toraji, in his private monthly magazine called Seisho chishiki (Biblical Knowledge).
25. In this regard the Mukyōkai movement is congruent with the ethos of ordinary Japanese people. However, this is the reason, I suspect, that Uchimura emphasized the need for "sanctification" of the Japanese bushidō.

many civil rights movements, including some "circle" activities, are usually not tightly bound by their organization.[26] Many Japanese seem to prefer loosely organized groups in which they can feel a heightened sense of participation without assuming binding responsibilities of formal group membership. Beheiren, a citizens' movement opposed to the Vietnam War, urged people to give support without joining officially, or establishing a formal organization. In this loose formation, there is room for both those who wish to involve themselves deeply and those who prefer a lesser commitment to the movement. This kind of loose and informal bond is comfortable for many Japanese; and it often works much better than a system of fixed official membership. Even today many writers in Japan do not make official contracts with their publishers. The absence of a formal contract is often considered to be a sign of personal trust, and publishers do not take unfair advantage of the situation. In college activities, too, many students prefer voluntary associations to officially organized athletic club activities.[27]

Voluntary, flexible, and occasional bonds seem to work more effectively for binding together many people, although there is also the possibility that such a group will be too unorganized, a problem that can be avoided by formal organization and contract. By this kind of flexible and voluntary group formation some Japanese seem to have avoided the dilemma of institutionalization. Here again, however, there is the danger of the institutionalization of the anti-institutional movements. This is why Uchimura tried to form only a spiritual group through the Mukyōkai meetings and to destroy again and again, and to form again and again, in a kind of permanent revolution. Uchimura and his followers have enjoyed the benefits of loose group formation and its warm personal relationship in their religious practices. It has been effective in group formation and also in preserving the solid tie among its members. This is why, perhaps, Uchimura's idea of a non-institutional Christian movement has attracted more followers in Japan than we can ascertain from a statistical investigation.[28]

For this ethos is also very dangerous in the sense that everybody can be free of official responsibility. Maruyama Masao characterized this ethos of the Japanese as "the system of irresponsibility."

26. By "circle activity" I mean an adult group activity centered on a common interest such as poetry reading, learning songs, etc.

27. Recently I learned that even in the United States, members of Nichiren Shōshū of America (Sōka gakkai) have small cell meetings called "district meetings," almost in the same style of those of Mukyōkai people. This might be a sign of an American version of Mukyōkai style. I have also met American couples who conduct family worship services, taking turns among themselves, since they became very disappointed with their church over its attitude

**Contrasts between the Institutional and Non-Institutional Approach**

When we think of Uchimura we cannot avoid reference to another important figure, Niishima Jō (1843-1890), who founded Dōshisha English School in 1875. In fact there is a revealing contrast between Uchimura and Niishima in regard to the effect of institutional and of non-institutional ways of group formation. Niishima contributed greatly to the development of Japanese education, and Dōshisha, the institution he founded, has grown to be one of the largest private schools in Japan, with more than twenty thousand students, ranging from junior high school to graduate school.[29] Dōshisha is truly a heritage left by Niishima, and he would be proud of its popularity and the productivity of its students today.

By contrast, Uchimura left nothing visible. His Bible Study Meeting was dispersed and his personal monthly magazine, Seisho no Kenkyū, which continued until its 357th issue, was, following his request, discontinued upon his death in March 1930. Above all, Uchimura built no Church as an institution.[30] He avoided everything institutional and left no physical monument to his memory when he died. He urged his close disciples to become independent, especially in his later years, and most of them became independent lay evangelists. All he left, therefore, were his books and papers. Interestingly enough, he once wrote in his diary that his books could be his Church.[31]

The respective positions of Niishima and Uchimura in Japanese society today afford an interesing comparison. Niishima's school, Dōshisha, has produced tremendous numbers of students over the last one hundred years. However, Niishima himself is usually regarded as simply the founder of one Christian college in early modern Japan, not as a significant Christian thinker or theologian. Dōshisha is almost completely secularized. Niishima's writings

toward the Vietnam War and other socio-political issues.

28. Here again we do not have accurate data concerning the present situation of Mukyōkai movements. Our only information comes by oral communication (kuchikomi), which seems to allow for more intimacy among the Mukyōkai Christians than official, impersonal means of communication.

29. After World War II, followers of Niishima even gave his name to a junior and senior high school built in Gumma Prefecture. Dōshisha maintains contact with Amherst College, where Niishima studied, through student and faculty exchange programs.

30. Strictly speaking, Uchimura helped in establishing the church in Takeoka, Chiba Prefecture, when he had to retreat because of the lese majesty affair in 1891.

31. "Hibi no shogai," April 18, 1919, Zenshū, XVII, p. 111.

might of course be read and praised by Dōshisha people, but his influence today appears quite limited outside such circles.

Uchimura had no desire to leave any disciples, but he seems nonetheless to have many anonymous followers throughout Japan. He is undoubtedly one of the best selling Christian writers in Japanese. His reputation stems partly from his followers' good leadership and intellectual standing and partly from his talent as a writer. Uchimura's followers provided moral leadership during the critical days of national discouragement and after World War II as well as during the period immediately following the war. They are remembered today not only because of their status as university professors and social workers, but also because some were jailed during World War II as pacifists. Uchimura's followers were unrecognizable unless they made public confessions. Yet few of them, whether intellectuals or non-intellectuals, who practiced the Christian way of life in those difficult days compromised their principles.[32]

Uchimura has followers not only among Mukyōkai Christians, but also among ordinary Church Christians. Since Uchimura was able to attract many bright young students to his Bible Study Meeting, he influenced many intellectuals through his lectures and books. During the period 1890-1930, especially, many college professors and novelists came under his influence.[33] Today there are more than fifty small Mukyōkai groups in Japan.[34] Moreover, there are at least three different editions of Uchimura's complete works.[35] Uchimura left no institution, but his books and papers are still alive in the hearts of many Japanese people.

Again we find a striking paradox in Uchimura's method of organizing. When he tried to dissolve his Sunday meeting and abolish his personal

32. Among these disciples were Yanaihara Tadao, Nambara Shigeru, Ebara Mari, Mitani Takamasa, Sekine Masao, Maeda Gorō, Kanda Tateo, Shinoto Yoshito, Otsuka Hisao, Fujita Wakao, etc.
33. Cf. Inagaki Manami, Uchimura o tsuida hitotachi (Uchimura's Follwers), Asahi Shimbunsha, 1976. Among hosts of writers and novelists in modern Japan we can name at least the following people who were personally influenced by Uchimura: Masamune Hakuchō, Shiga Naoya, Osanai Kaoru, Arishima Takeo, Kunikida Doppo, Nagayo Yoshio, Nakazato Kaizan.
34. Cf. Kirisutokyō nenkan, (Kirisuto Shimbunsha, 1976).
35. Uchimura Kanzō zenshū (Iwanami shoten, 1932-33), 20 vols.; Uchimura Kanzō chosakushū (Iwanami shoten, 1953-55), 21 vols.; and Uchimura Kanzō shinkō chosaku zenshū (Kyōbunkan, 1960-73), 25 vols. See also Uchimura Kanzō seisho chūshaku zenshū, 17 vols.; Uchimura Kanzō nikki shokan zenshū, 8 vols.; Uchimura Kanzō eibun chosaku zenshū, 7 vols.

magazines, he only strengthened the ties of his followers. For by giving up his personal magazines and abandoning Sunday meetings, his followers were presented with the task of starting another meeting consisting of almost the same members. The greater the effort to reform the group, the stronger the personal ties seem to become. Whether it is characteristic of Japanese groups to flourish in the face of adversity is difficult to say. But the result of dissolving Mukyōkai groups is clear: they reform with even stronger links than before.

By firmly denying immediate continuity, Mukyōkai members are in fact paradoxically confirming their religious ties, and are affirming dialectical continuity. They may quit meeting and stop publishing their magazines or pamphlets; but eventually they try them once again, even more earnestly, with stronger passion and a similar method. I am not certain whether Uchimura himself was aware of this paradoxical result; I am simply stating my observation of the effects of this kind of frequent dissolution.

Many followers of Uchimura seem to have maintained their religious zeal in this kind of flexible way for considerable periods of time. This appears to be congruent with the psychology of the Japanese people. The rise and fall of group formation over the course of time can also be found in other fields. For instance it is seen in politics, military groups, and in the bureaucracy: when the boss or the leader resigns or dies, the people who are left cannot maintain the group by themselves. They often first disband completely, then try to organize a similar group.

Thus by focusing on non-institutional religious faith, Uchimura seems to have tapped a powerful force in the Japanese mentality. That is, by emphasizing the permanence of their faith and teacher, Uchimura could make his followers' faith stronger and their organization tighter whenever he tried to discontinue their meetings or magazines. Here the spirit of lamenting the "evanescence" of life is tactfully (though unconsciously) used. The Japanese seem to believe in the recuperative power of history, and understand their "dependence on time" (jikan o ate ni suru) as assuring that they can try again in the future.[36]

A final contrast between Uchimura and Niishima can be seen in their attitudes towards foreign missionaries. Niishima worked closely with many

36. Ohara Shin, "Time as Japanese Civil Religion: Some Social and Philosophical Implications of the Japanese Awareness of Time and Season," Look Japan, September 10 and October 10, 1979.

foreign missionaries and got along well with them. In contrast, Uchimura refused to recognize their leadership or accept their guidance. Consistent with his notion of Mukyōkai, Uchimura recognized no established line of Christian authority and even tried to abolish the simple succession of the Christian faith through his disciples. Because of his fierce spirit of independence and decisiveness, Uchimura seems paradoxically to have succeeded in renewing a sense of faith. Perhaps because of this he could preserve this sense of faith fresh and strong throughout his life. Followers of Uchimura also seem to imitate this tendency, which interestingly enough, corresponds to the traditional ethos of the Japanese people as well.

## "Tuning West" by "Turning East"

Uchimura helped many people become Christian in a country which had few Christians. Converts to Christianity in Japan often experienced severe societal pressures. But somehow many have managed to survive in the religiously plural society, preserving their subjective non-traditional faith even without the support of formal church organization. Does the example of Uchimura and his churchless Christianity provide Americans with a solution to the religious dilemma which they face today? Does the Japanese experience with Mukyōkai hold any lessons for Americans? Uchimura emphasized the possibility of being a Christian in a religiously pluralistic and religiously indifferent situation. He said that one can become a Christian without having buildings, registration, or professional clergy; and he showed that one can be religious without displaying the trappings of religion. He was especially critical of the patrimonial and secularized temples and shrines in Japan and believed that they had lost their vital meaning in the religious life of most people. While equally critical of the churches in Christianity, he believed he had found through his churchless movement a way of preserving the faith while abandoning the formal trappings of his new religion.

As Americans' confidence in their own greatness and world leadership has weakened, many university students and other young Americans are turning East for religious guidance to Zen Buddhism, Yoga, Hare Krishna and other similar groups. Many go to Japan today not to teach their way of life and religion as the missionaries did in Uchimura's day, but to learn about Japanese religion and society.[37] By turning East, many Americans are following the

37. For instance. E. F. Schumacher, <u>Small is Beautiful</u> (Harper and Row, 1973), discusses the theme of Buddhist economics in relation to ecology.

same tortuous route which Uchimura and other Japanese took in becoming Christians in the late nineteenth century. Like Niishima and Uchimura, young Americans who become followers of the Hare Krishna movement, for instance, are creating serious conflicts with their families and society. For many Americans this is the first serious disruption in their history of Judeo-Christianity. While the United States is often referred to as a pluralistic society, Americans have been pluralistic only in terms of ethnicity, not religion. For this reason, the case of Uchimura may have more significance for Americans today than ever before. In another sense, too, Uchimura's teachings and his Mukyōkai movement may be meaningful to Americans who have lost interest in their church. He has shown how one can become a Christian without having any church affiliation and how one can keep one's faith without any church buildings.

Recently Harvard theologian Harvey Cox has noticed the tendency of many Americans to "turn East." According to Cox, it is now time for Westerners to learn more from the East.[38] This is exactly what Uchimura prophesized in the late nineteenth century. In a well-known article in 1892 entitled "Japan: Its Mission," Uchimura expressed confidence that Japan could contribute something to the future of humanity in the field of religion rather than in such fields as weaponry or economics. He believed, moreover, that Japan had a special opportunity through religion to bring about a reconciliation between East and West:

> Japan's mission may be multifarious; but the one we have laid much stress upon is grand enough to call forth the highest aspiration of the nation. To reconcile the East with the West; to be the advocate of the East and the harbinger of the West; this we believe to be the mission which Japan is called upon to fulfill.[39]

Thirty years later, he wrote again about the mission of the Japanese and concluded that just as they had preserved Buddhism and Confucianism so too could they preserve Christianity for mankind.[40] Christianity, which was

38. Harvey Cox, Turning East (1977). Also Ezra F. Vogel's, Japan as Number One (1979). The former analyzes the recent religious influence on America by Japan and Asia, whereas the latter focuses on Japan's potential contribution to the world as a social model.
39. "The Japan Daily Mail," February 5, 1892, in Zenshū, XVI, pp. 15-26. Also, Carl Michalson, Japanese Contribution to Christian Theology. (The Westminster Press, 1960).
40. "Nihon no tenshoku" (The Mission of Japan), in Zenshū, XIV, pp. 591-600.

born in Judea and spread first to Europe and then to America, had came to Japan through America. But in its historical travels it had become either a secularized business or a professionalized institution and in the process had lost its genuine spirit. Uchimura's point was that after Christianity was abandoned in Christian countries, as Buddhism had been in India and Confucianism in China, the Japanese will preserve, revive and propagate it in a new form: namely, in the Mukyōkai style—without any buildings or any official memberships. For Uchimura the Japanese people were the champions of that purpose. "That Japan is the divine nation and the Japanese are spiritual people," he wrote, "is not self-praising words," but a statement of their historical mission.[41]

Uchimura might have exaggerated the mission of the Japanese, but his prophecy is not far off the mark. As many Americans have begun to "turn East" in their religious lives, and to encounter polytheism for the first time, they may learn two important lessons from Uchimura and his churchless Christianity: first, how to keep their subjective faith amidst religious pluralism in a seeming pagan society; and second, how to preserve their faith without the support of the church. The church no longer holds a central position in the hearts of most Americans.[42] They are less confident of their traditional faith. Many of them are eager to learn more about non-Christian religions and seem less Christ-centered. They have even started to display a willingness to accept different religious heritages and thereby to develop a true religious pluralism.

A new religious relativism is emerging not only in Asia, where people are used to a plural religious heritage, but also in the traditionally Christian countries as well. Thus Americans are becoming aware of the need to revise their religious tradition, in particular their monotheism and rigid institutionalism. Harvey Cox is right in calling this tendency "turning East." The question remains, however, how Americans can preserve their Christian faith without their church. So far they seem to be able to maintain their faith only when they are affiliated with the institution of the church. Here is an essential difference between Uchimura's Mukyōkai followers of Japan and the churchless people in the United States. Uchimura's serious and sensitive concern with the development of a non-institutional faith may prove to be significant for Americans. For although most are unaware of his teachings now, they

41. Zenshū, XIV, p. 598.
42. See Marie Augusta Neal, A Socio-Theology of Letting Go (New York: Paulist Press, 1977).

may eventually become less dependent on institutional Christianity and accept more pluralism in their lives. It would indeed be an irony of history if American descendents of such New England lay Christians as Seelye and Clark were to be reminded of their own religious heritage by the followers of Uchimura Kanzō.

Some of the recent American interest in non-Christian religions may turn out to be superficial. But even if this is the case, it is nevertheless quite clear that Americans have lost their previous zeal for their own institutionalized religious heritage. Yet they are turning to the east without sufficiently tuning in the west. This is why, it seems to me, they are not yet aware of the validity of Uchimura's idea of preserving subjective faith in a non-institutional setting. They are no longer interested in churches; but they seek to satisfy their strong religious urge by incorporating non-Christian traditions. Americans today are undergoing a spiritual struggle in trying to reconcile various forms of religious consciousness. They have seriously begun their quest for religious relativism.

It is in this religiously chaotic situation that I find great relevance for Uchimura's idea of Mukyōkai. Despite its origins in Japan, his thought is universally applicable. Characterized by religious relativism and a non-institutional form, Mukyōkai nevertheless allows for—in fact, strengthens—one's religious faith. Thus, rather than lament the growing relativism and decline of institutionalized religion in America, I would point to the Japanese experience with the Mukyōkai movement and emphasize the positive and creative potential of current religious trends.

# BIBLIOGRAPHY

Arima, Tatsuo. 1961. Uchimura Kanzō: A study of the post-Meiji Japanese intelligentsia. Papers on Japan 1:130-88.

____________. 1969. Uchimura Kanzō: The politics of spiritual despair. In Tatsuo Arima, The failure of freedom: A portrait of modern Japanese intellectuals. Cambridge: Harvard University Press.

Bremer, Shella. 1960. The life and thought of Uchimura Kanzō during the period 1888-1900. Unpublished thesis, International Christian University.

Brunner, Emil. 1959. A unique Christian mission: The Mukyōkai (Non-Church) movement in Japan. In Walter Leibrech (ed.), Religion and culture: Essays in honor of Paul Tillich. New York: Harper and Bros.

____________. 1959. Die christliche Nichtkirchlichebewegung in Japan. Evangelische Theologie 4:147-55.

Bryant, Gladys Eugenia. 1971. American Congregational missionaries and social reform in Meiji Japan (1870-1900). Unpublished dissertation, Vanderbilt University.

Burkle, Howard R. 1962. Uchimura Kanzō: Christian transcendentalist. Japan Christian Quarterly 28:115-24.

Caldarola, Carlo. 1972. Japanese reaction to the institutional church. Journal of Ecumenical Studies 9:489-520.

____________. 1971. Non-church Christianity in Japan: Western Christianity and Japan's cultural identity. Unpublished dissertation, University of California, Berkeley.

____________. 1973. Non-church Christianity in Japan: Western Christianity and Japan's cultural identity. International Journal of Contemporary Sociology 10:236-47.

____________. 1979. Christianity: The Japanese way. Leiden: Brill.

Cary, Otis. 1957. Kanzō Uchimura. Amherst Alumni News, July.

____________. 1956. Uchimura, Neesima and Amherst--recently discovered correspondence. Japan Quarterly, 3:439-59.

Chard, Margaret Joan. 1968. Uchimura Kanzō and his influence on Christianity in Japan. Unpublished M.A. thesis, Columbia University.

Dohi, Akio. 1960. Uchimura's conception of the church. Studies in the Christian Religion, October.

Doi, Takeo. 1980. Uchimura Kanzō: Japanese Christianity in comparative perspective. In Albert M. Craig (ed.), Japan: A comparative view. Princeton: Princeton University Press.

Drummond, Richard. 1965. The non-church movement in Japan: An introduction. Journal of Ecumenical Studies 2:448-51.

Germany, Charles H. 1965. Protestant theologies in modern Japan. Tokyo: IISR Press.

Hagiwara, Itsue. 1962. No-church movement: Ein Vergleich des Kirchenbegriffs von Sebastian Franck und Kanzo Utschimura. Marburg: Nolte.

Hiranuma, Toshio. 1958. Amherst and Uchimura: One American contribution to Japan. Jinbun Ronkyū 2:1-14.

Hori, Mitsuo. 1963. Kanzō Uchimura—Baumeister der ungebauten Kirche (Mukyōkai). Stuttgart.

Howes, John F. 1954. Kanzō Uchimura: The formative years. Japan Christian Quarterly 20:194-208.

____________. 1957. Kanzō Uchimura: Teacher and writer. Japan Christian Quarterly 23:150-56.

____________. 1957. Kanzō Uchimura: Social reformer. Japan Christian Quarterly 23:243-52.

____________. 1958. Kanzō Uchimura on war. Japan Christian Quarterly 24:290-92.

____________. 1957. The non-church Christian movement in Japan. Transactions of the Asiatic Society of Japan, 3rd series, 5:119-37.

____________. 1958. Two works by Uchimura Kanzō until recently unknown in Japan. Transactions of the International Conference of Orientalists in Japan 3:25-31.

____________. 1960. Uchimura Kanzō and traditional Japanese religions. Japanese Religions 2:23-30.

____________. 1960. Uchimura Kanzō on Christopher Columbus. Japan Christian Quarterly 26:239-45.

____________. 1960. The chijinron of Uchimura Kanzō. Transactions of the International Conference of Orientalists in Japan, Tokyo.

____________. 1964. Uchimura Kanzō, a Christian and a Japanese. In Ryusaku Tsunoda et al. (eds. and translators), Sources of Japanese tradition, Vol. 2.

____________. 1965. Japanese Christians and American missionaries. In Marius B. Jansen (ed.), Changing Japanese attitudes toward modernization. Princeton: Princeton University Press.

____________. 1965. Western words and Japanese pre-occupations: The English-language works of Uchimura Kanzō. Pacific Affairs 38:307-325.

____________. 1965. Japan's enigma: The young Uchimura Kanzō. Unpublished dissertation, Columbia University.

____________. 1966. Two types: Kagawa and Uchimura. Theology Today 23:88-97.

____________. 1967. Japanese protestant stereotypes and the role of the missionary. Japan Christian Quarterly 33:151-60.

____________. 1968. Uchimura Kanzō. Encyclopedia Britannica 22:457-58.

____________. 1970. Uchimura Kanzō: Japanese prophet. In Dankwart Rustow (ed.), Philosophers and kings, studies in leadership. New York: G. Braziller.

____________. 1978. Uchimura Kanzō: the Bible and war. In Nobuya Bamba and John F. Howes (eds.), Pacifism in Japan: the Christian and socialist tradition. Kyoto: Minerva Press.

Jennings, Raymond P. 1958. Jesus, Japan, and Kanzō Uchimura. Tokyo: Kyōbunkan.

____________. 1956. The view of the church of Kanzō Uchimura and its significance for Japanese Christianity. Unpublished dissertation, Berkeley Baptist Divinity School.

Jorgenson, Arthur. 1927. Dominant ideas in Mr. Uchimura's writing. Kaitakusha, February, 1-4.

____________. 1927. Is the Christian church Christian? Kaitakusha, July, 1-4.

Kakihara, Seiichiro. 1937. Uchimura the prophet. Japan Christian Quarterly 3:22-28.

Kishimoto, Hideo (ed.). 1956. Japanese religion in the Meiji era. Translated and adapted by John F. Howes. Tokyo: Ōbunsha.

Kitagawa, Daisuke. 1961. No-church Christianity in Japan. Occasional Paper No. 8. London: Department of Missionary Studies, International Missionary Council.

Koike, Naoshi. 1965. Kanzō Uchimura: A summary of his life and faith. Memoirs of Muroran Institute of Technology 5:1.

Koike, Tatsuo. 1963. Protestantismus in Japan und Grundlegung zur Theologie des Durchbruchs. Tokyo: Proceedings of the Department of Foreign Languages and Literatures, University of Tokyo.

Kraemer, Hendrik. 1938. The Christian message in a non-christian world. New York: Harper and Bros.

Kunimoto, Yoshirō. 1972. The complete works of Uchimura Kanzō. Japan Quarterly 19:491ff.

Lee, Robert. 1974. Religious evolution and the individuation of the self in Japanese history. Unpublished dissertation, Harvard University.

____________. 1977. The individuation of the self in Japanese history. Japanese Journal of Religious Studies 4:4-39.

Maeda, Gorō. 1951. Churchless Christianity. Japan Christian Yearbook, 181ff.

____________. 1966. Kanzō Uchimura and his legacy. Philosophical Studies of Japan 7:97-110.

Maruyama, Masao. 1966. Fukuzawa, Uchimura, and Okakura. Developing Economies 4:594-611.

Masaike, Jin. 1964-1968. The life of Uchimura Kanzō. In The lure of the Litchfield Hills 26:12.

Michalson, Carl. 1960. Japanese contributions to Christian theology. Philadelphia: The Westminster Press.

Miwa, Kimitada. 1967. Crossroads of patriotism in imperial Japan: Shiga Shigetaka (1863-1927), Uchimura Kanzō (1861-1930), and Nitobe Inazō (1862-1933). Unpublished dissertation, Princeton University.

Miyabe, Kingō. 1937. An outline life of Kanzō Uchimura. Japan Christian Quarterly 3:15ff.

Miyata, Mitsuo. 1964. Der politische Auftrag des japanischen Protestantismus. Hamburg: H. Reich.

Nakazawa, Kōki. 1951. The essence and development of non-church in Japan. Unpublished paper, Union Theological Seminary.

____________. 1952. Prophets and the destiny of their country. Unpublished paper, Union Theological Seminary.

____________. 1952. The mukyōkai or non-church movement in Japan. Occasional Bulletin of the Missionary Research Library.

____________. 1954. Churchless Christianity in Japan. Japan Christian Yearbook, 154-59.

____________. 1968. The future of Christianity: From the point of view of a non-church Christian professor. Japan Christian Yearbook, 164-68.

Norman, W. H. H. 1958. An interim report on mukyōkai-shugi today. Kwansei Gakuin University Annual Studies. (Reprinted from The International Review of Missions October, 1959, 380-93.)

____________. 1963. Kanzō Uchimura--founder of non-church movement. Contemporary Religions in Japan 4:264-74, 332-50.

____________. 1961. Uchimura Kanzō's quest for salvation. Unpublished ms.

Okazaki, Yoshie (ed.). 1955. Japanese literature in the Meiji era. Translated and adapted by V. H. Viglielmo. Tokyo: Ōbunsha.

Prichard, Marianna and Norman. 1967. Ten against the storm. New York: Friendship Press.

Rahn, David Philip. 1971. Uchimura Kanzō and Nitobe Inazō: A biographical study of Japanese Christianity and culture. Unpublished M.A. thesis, University of Michigan.

Rhodes, Erroll F. 1966. A New Year's dream (translation of Uchimura's Hatsuyume). In Nakazawa Ikuko, Gendai ni ikiru Uchimura Kanzō. Tokyo: Hirokawa Shoten.

Rosenkranz, Gerhard. 1962. Utschimura Kanzo. Die Religion in Geschichte und Gegenwart, 3rd ed., vol. 6, 1222ff. Tübingen: Mohr.

Sekine, Masao. 1971. Die Geschichte der japanischen Christenheit und die Bibelwissenschaft. Evangelische Missionszeitschrift, 145-53.

Shionoya, Satoshi. 1970. Kanzō Uchimura's view of missions. Tenri Journal of Religion, 79-97.

Shimo, Mochinobu. 1970. New England Congregationalism and the modernization of Japan in the period of the Meiji, 1868-1912. Unpublished dissertation, Boston University.

Suzuki, Toshiro. 1952. The non-church group. Japan Christian Quarterly 18:136-43.

Takagi, Yasaka. 1956. Uchimura Kanzō--prophet, patriot, Christian. Japan Quarterly, 431-39.

Thomas, Winburn T. 1959. Protestant beginnings in Japan. Tokyo: Tuttle.

Yanaihara, Tadao. 1948. Religion and democracy in Japan. Japan Institute for Pacific Studies. Tokyo: Tokyo University Press.

MICHIGAN PAPERS IN JAPANESE STUDIES

No. 1. Political Leadership in Contemporary Japan, edited by Terry MacDougall.

No. 2. Parties, Candidates and Voters in Japan; Six Quantitative Studies, edited by John Creighton Campbell.

No. 3. The Japanese Automobile Industry: Model and Challenge for the Future?, edited by Robert E. Cole.

No. 4. Survey of Japanese Collections in the United States, 1979-1980, by Naomi Fukuda.

No. 5. Culture and Religion in Japanese-American Relations: Essays on Uchimura Kanzō, 1861-1930, edited by Ray A. Moore.

No. 6. Sukeroku's Double Identity: The Dramatic Structure of Edo Kabuki, by Barbara E. Thornbury.